T0381064

LOVE AND SEX

Are we ever too old?

NIELI LANGER

Order this book online at www.trafford.com
or email orders@trafford.com

Most Trafford titles are also available at major online book retailers.

Print information available on the last page.

ISBN: 978-1-4120-9460-3 (sc)
ISBN: 978-1-4669-7966-6 (e)

Trafford rev. 08/08/2023

www.trafford.com
North America & international
toll-free: 844-688-6899 (USA & Canada)
fax: 812 355 4082

To My Oded

Your smile was an invitation for my imagination to go wild. Then began a journey together by two different people from two different worlds starting at forever and ending at never…

Nieli
May 2006

TABLE OF CONTENTS

The fires still burn...

You are walking through a park during the daylight hours, when you come upon two persons sitting on a park bench. They are kissing and hugging, totally immersed in one another and completely oblivious to anyone or anything around them. Upon looking closer, you find they are a young man and a young woman... an old man and an old woman... an old man and a young woman... an old woman and a young man... two women... two men.[1]

By the way, does it really matter?

Love is a word, a knowing look, a quiet walk, a cozy feeling. Love that is good takes thinking through and living with. Mature love says: "I need you because I love you." Immature love says: "I love you because I need you." In *The Art of Loving*, Erich Fromm wrote that if love is art then it requires knowledge and effort. AND, mastery of this art requires a person's whole attention, i.e., "there must be nothing else in the world more important than the art."[2] If love is only a feeling that can come and go, then there is no basis for the promise to love one another forever. Love requires commitment, care, responsibility and respect. Therefore, love is a universal human emotion whose expression may be experienced throughout the life cycle. As the Beatles have reminded us,

"All you need is love, all you need is love; all you need is love, love, love is all you ever need."[3]

Sex is a primary human drive and can be considered alongside thirst, hunger, and avoidance of pain. We are sexual beings from birth to death. Older people *can* and *do* make love although there may be decreased levels of arousal and a lessening in intensity, along with a slowing down of response. Yes, older couples still desire each other much as they always have yet we need to accept that *some* older people are not as interested in sex now as when they were young. Even though sex for older people may not be quantitatively identical to that experienced by younger people, older couples' need for sexual expression endures.

Sexual intimacy between couples involves mutual affection, respect and trust. Sexual desire refers to a person's interest in being sexual and is the interaction of drive, personal values, and motivation. Sexual drive is typically manifested by sexual thoughts, feelings, fantasies, genital tingling and seeking out sexual activity. As they age, most men and women still desire sexual intimacy although they *may* experience a decrease of sexual drive.

The second component of desire reflects an individual's expectations, beliefs and values about sexual activity. The more positive the person's beliefs and values are about sexuality, the greater the person's desire to engage in sexual activities. Psychological and interpersonal enthusiasm is part of a person's desire and helps him/her decide if to behave sexually with a given partner. The significance of an elder's need for sexual intimacy is entirely dependent on what it means to that individual. ***Being sexually active or inactive is not an issue of normal or dysfunctional behavior.*** For example, if a woman has lost some of her drive but remains motivated to be close and intimate with her partner, then despite having little physical cues or interest, she still enjoys the sexual experience.

The level of sexual intimacy among older couples will likely increase as Baby Boomers age. Baby Boomers reached adulthood when safe, effective contraceptive methods became widely accepted and accessible, thereby encouraging earlier and more frequent sexual activity for self-expression and pleasure rather than for reproductive function alone. A more open-minded attitude about sex compounded by the sheer number of people in this cohort suggests that the subject of sexual intimacy will be prominent in the lives of older couples as well as for their families, eventual care providers and society at large.

Yes

"Do you still want me?" you asked.
And I said, "You don't have to ask me every day.
You said, "Well, do you?"
And I said, "Yes."
But what I really said within my heart was,
"Want him?"
Do I want him?
In an exotic, quixotic way
I want him.
I want him because
I can walk with him,
And he talks to me about the things I like to talk about.
And he says funny things to me,
And sometimes he thinks they're so funny
He says them twice.
And I know him better than
Any woman has any right to know a man.
And with all that I find
Just when I think I know him best,
I know him not at all.
And all I really want is a chance to know him better,
And that takes time.
And I would like to take all the time given me
To know him better
Which is the real reason
I cannot bear to be away from him.
"Yes."[4]

— Lois Wyse 1967

Sexuality is a fundamental dimension of all human beings; it is a statement of being alive. It goes beyond the sexual urge and the sex act. It is not only a physical need but also an important component in the development of each individual. It gives concrete expression to the desire for an increasingly exclusive relationship with a partner. Sexuality refers to an individual's self-perception of being attractive as a sexual partner. The ways we dress, speak to others and daydream are all affected by sexuality and sexual identity. For older people, it often provides the opportunity to express not only passion but also affection, loyalty and esteem.

An essential part of psychological well-being for older adults is their interest in and ability to express their sexuality, regardless of physical or mental health. Sexuality includes more than just physical activities. Sexuality in middle and later life reflects sexual identity, emotional and physical response and maturity, as well as personal attitudes and social norms. Sexuality is an affirmation of being alive.

True sexual intimacy is achievable only by individuals who have the capacity for emotional intimacy. There is no age at which sexual activities, thoughts, or desires must end although the way in which sexuality is expressed may change. Sex doesn't necessarily get better or worse with aging; it's just different. Genital contact my become less frequent but interest, pleasure and frequency of non-intercourse activities such as caressing, embracing and kissing may remain stable or increase as people get older. Older adults are sexual people even in the face of typical and extraordinary changes in functioning. Throughout the life cycle, the ability to experience warmth, caring, physical intimacy and connection to significant others contributes to an adult's self-esteem.

Belonging for an older couple signifies identification as a couple, sharing of values, comfortable interaction, and a sense of safety and security. Lummis Indians of the Pacific Northwest saw old age as the proper time to fall in love. "It was the proper time to suffer romances, and jealousy, and lose your head – old age, when you felt things more, and could spare the time to go dead nuts over a person, and understand how fine a thing it was."[5]

Esther and Al Kline in their apartment, Miami Beach, Florida[6]

Someday, after we have mastered the winds, the waves,
the tides and gravity, we shall harness the energies of
love. Then, for the second time in the history of the
world, man will have discovered fire.[7]

—Pierre Teilhard de Chardin

It is impossible to define aging only in chronological terms, contrary to the messages on birthday cards that seem to imply that aging starts at age 40 or 65. An active aging perspective implies that aging is a lifelong process in which changes take place in the organism throughout the life span: good, bad and neutral. Aging is a complex process that involves many different factors such as cultural, ethnic, and gender differences and is unique to each individual. Love, sexual intimacy and sexuality are matters that help define us and often contribute to how well we will continue to live and age.

Enhanced knowledge and healthy attitudes toward sexuality can help dispel negative myths, stereotypes, and self-fulfilling attitudes in older people and the general public about sexual needs and feelings in later life. They can help promote the perception that full sexual expression is part of the entire extent of adulthood.

What is your Sexual IQ?

The following is a scale for the assessment of knowledge and attitudes about sexuality in the older person. The correct answers to the knowledge questions appear at the end of the questionnaire with rules for scoring. Questions related to attitude follow but no answers are provided.

Aging Sexual Attitudes and Knowledge Scale[8]

Knowledge Questions:

*1. Sexual activity in aged persons is often dangerous to their health
.1 True   .2 False   .3 Don't know

2. Males over the age of 65 typically take longer to attain an erection
.1 True   .2 False   .3 Don't know

3. Males over the age of 65 usually experience a reduction in intensity of orgasm relative to younger males
.1 True   .2 False   .3 Don't know

4. The firmness of erection in aged males is often less than that of younger males
.1 True   .2 False   .3 Don't know

*Indicates that the scoring should be reversed such that 2=1, and 1=2, i.e., a low score indicates high knowledge

5. The older female (65+ years of age) has reduced vaginal lubrication secretion relative to younger females

      .1 True   .2 False   .3 Don't know

6. The aged female takes longer to achieve adequate vaginal lubrication relative to younger females

      .1 True   .2 False   .3 Don't know

7. The older female may experience painful intercourse due to reduced elasticity of the vagina and reduced vaginal lubrication

      .1 True   .2 False   .3 Don't know

8. Sexuality is typically a life-long need.

      .1 True   .2 False   .3 Don't know

9. Sexual behavior in older people (65+) increases the risk of heart attack.

      .1 True   .2 False   .3 Don't know

*10. Most males over the age of 65 are unable to engage in sexual intercourse

      .1 True   .2 False   .3 Don't know

11. Relatively speaking, the most sexually active younger people tend to become the most sexually active older people

      .1 True   .2 False   .3 Don't know

12. There is evidence that sexual activity in older persons has beneficial physical effects on the participants

      .1 True   .2 False   .3 Don't know

13. Sexual activity may be psychologically beneficial to older person participants

      .1 True   .2 False   .3 Don't know

*14. Most older females are sexually unresponsive

      .1 True   .2 False   .3 Don't know

15. The sex urge typically increases with age in males over 65

      .1 True   .2 False   .3 Don't know

16. Prescription drugs may alter a person's sex drive

      .1 True   .2 False   .3 Don't know

17. Females, after menopause, have a physiologically induced need for sexual activity

      .1 True   .2 False   .3 Don't know

18. Basically, changes with advanced age (65+) in sexuality involve a slowing of response time rather than a reduction of interest in sex

      .1 True   .2 False   .3 Don't know

19. Older males typically experience a reduced need to ejaculate and maintain an erection of the penis for a longer time than younger males

      .1 True   .2 False   .3 Don't know

*20. Older males and females cannot act as sex partners as both need younger partners for stimulation

      .1 True   .2 False   .3 Don't know

21. The most common determinant of the frequency of sexual activity in older couples is the interest or lack of interest of the husband in a sexual relationship with his wife

      .1 True   .2 False   .3 Don't know

22. Barbiturates, tranquilizers and alcohol may lower the sexual arousal levels of aged persons and interfere with sexual responsiveness

      .1 True   .2 False   .3 Don't know

23. Sexual disinterest in aged persons may be a reflection of a psychological state of depression
  .1 True   .2 False   .3 Don't know

24. There is a decrease in frequency of sexual activity with older age in males
  .1 True   .2 False   .3 Don't know

25. There is a greater decrease in male sexuality with age than there is in female sexuality
  .1 True   .2 False   .3 Don't know

26. Heavy consumption of cigarettes may diminish sexual desire
  .1 True   .2 False   .3 Don't know

27. An important factor in the maintenance of sexual responsiveness in the aging male is the consistency of sexual activity throughout his life
  .1 True   .2 False   .3 Don't know

28. Fear of the inability to perform sexually may bring about an inability to perform sexually in older males
  .1 True   .2 False   .3 Don't know

29. The ending of sexual activity in old age is most likely and primarily due to social and psychological causes rather than biological and physical causes
  .1 True   .2 False   .3 Don't know

*30. Excessive masturbation may bring about an early onset of mental confusion and dementia in the aged
  .1 True   .2 False   .3 Don't know

*31. There is an inevitable loss of sexual satisfaction in post-menopausal women
  .1 True   .2 False   .3 Don't know

32. Secondary (or non-physiologically caused) impotence increases in males over the age of 60 relative to younger males

      .1 True   .2 False   .3 Don't know

33. Impotence in aged males may literally be effectively treated and cured in many instances

      .1 True   .2 False   3. Don't know

34. In the absence of severe physical disability males and females may maintain sexual interest and activity well into their 80s and 90s

      .1 True   .2 False   .3 Don't know

35. Masturbation in older males and females has beneficial effects on the maintenance of sexual responsiveness

      .1 True   .2 False   .3 Don't know

ANSWERS: 1. False; 2. True; 3. True; 4. True; 5. True; 6. True; 7. True; 8. True; 9. False; 10. False; 11. True; 12. True; 13. True; 14. False; 15. False; 16. True; 17. False; 18. True; 19. True; 20. False; 21. True; 22. True; 23. True; 24. True; 25. True; 26. True; 27. True; 28. True; 29. True; 30. False; 31. False; 32. True; 33. True; 34. True; 35. True

Attitude Questions

(Seven point Likert Scale, Disagree=1; Agree=7)
Disagree 1-2-3-4-5-6-7 Agree

The following statements test your attitudes.
No answers are provided:

36.   Aged people have little interest in sexuality. (Aged = 65+ years of age). _____

37. An aged person who shows sexual interest brings disgrace to himself/herself._____

38. Institutions, such as nursing homes, ought not to encourage or support sexual activity of any sort in its residents._____

39. Male and female residents of nursing homes ought to live on separate floors or separate wings of the nursing home._____

40. Nursing homes have no obligation to provide adequate privacy for residents who desire to be alone, either by themselves or as a couple._____

41. As one becomes older (say past 65) interest in sexuality inevitably disappears_____

For items 42, 43, and 44: If an elderly relative of mine, living in a nursing home, was to have a sexual relationship with another resident, I would:

42. Complain to the management_____

43. Move my relative from this institution_____

+44. Stay out of it as it is not my concern_____

45. If I knew that a particular nursing home permitted and supported sexual activity in residents who desired such, I would not place a relative in that nursing home_____

46. It is immoral for older persons to engage in recreational sex_____

+47. I would like to know more about the changes in sexual functioning in the older years_____

+48. I feel I know all I need to know about sexuality in the aged_____

49. I would complain to the management if I knew of sexual activity between any residents of a nursing home_____

+50. I would support sex education courses for aged residents of nursing homes_____

+51. I would support sex education classes for the staff of nursing homes_____

+52. Masturbation is an acceptable activity for older males_____

+53. Masturbation is an acceptable sexual activity for older females_____

+54. Institutions, such as nursing homes, ought to provide large enough beds for couples who desire to sleep together_____

+55. Staff of nursing homes ought to be trained or educated with regard to sexuality in the aged and/or disabled_____

56. Residents of nursing homes ought not to engage in sexual activity of any sort_____

+57. Institutions, such as nursing homes, should provide opportunities for the social interaction of men and women_____

58. Masturbation is harmful and ought to be avoided_____

+59. Institutions, such as nursing homes, should provide privacy such as to allow the residents to engage in sexual behavior without fear of intrusion or observation_____

60. If family members object to a widowed relative engaging in sexual relations with another resident of a nursing home, it is the obligation of the management and staff to make certain that such sexual activity is prevented_____

61.   Sexual relations outside the context of marriage are always wrong_____

+Reverse scoring on items indicated such that 1=7, 7=1; 6=2, 2=6; 3=5, 5=3; 4 unchanged. A low scored indicates a permissive attitude.

People begin to understand their sexual identify very early in childhood. They mature sexually with puberty, but human sexuality continues throughout the life cycle, taking different forms depending on an individual's preferences and opportunities. Sexual behavior, because of the powerful role it plays in the lives of most people, is especially likely to be affected by:

- the physical and social environment, especially the availability of sexual partners and privacy
- the interactions of physical and mental health changes
- the individual's self-concept/self-esteem and desire for intimacy
- religious teachings and attitudes expressed or implied by parents as we grow up and by adult children as we age

Sexuality is one of the least understood aspects of aging. An old saying pertaining to sexuality and aging states: "We think our parents are too old to; we think our kids are too young to; our kids think we are too old to; so who in the heck is supposed to?" The best response is: everyone who wants to experience positive, ongoing sexuality throughout the life cycle.

Although our society is increasingly tolerant of safe sex for nearly every segment of our population, it often seems to imply that sexuality does not have a place in the lives of older people. The absence of attention in the literature and in the public forum to sexuality as a quality-of-life issue for older adults seems to contradict the growing emphasis in health promotion on viewing health from a wellness perspective across the life span.

Widespread stereotypes can negatively affect an older person's sexual experience especially when adult children and grandchildren often convey the message that sex is shameful and perverse for older adults. Adult children seeing parents on the permanently disabled list cannot imagine that they were once great sluggers.

What I thought I knew about love and sex And really don't...

Myths are created to explain what we don't understand. As unlikely as a myth may sound to our reality, it appeals to our emotions. Myths fed by misinformation surround late-life sexuality. The presumption is that older people do not have sexual desires; they are physically incapable of making love even if they wanted to; older people are physically unattractive and, therefore, undesirable; older people who are sexually active are weird or deviant. Therefore, an older woman who shows an evident interest in sex is often labeled "oversexed" or pathetically clinging to her youth. These myths form the basis for many comments that poke fun or trigger disdain at sexuality in older adults.

The socio-cultural context in which older adults were raised and the prevailing cultural stereotypes, misconceptions, and jokes about old age and sexuality can negatively influence older adults' attitudes toward sexuality and sexual activity. Societal standards of physical appearance and beauty also influence sexuality. A double standard still seems to exist pertaining to men and women and the aging process. Men are victims of a lifelong excessive emphasis on physical performance. Being masculine has been equated with the frequency and potency of their sexual performance in comparison with younger men. Nevertheless, in other situations, men are described as gray and distinguished, while women as moving farther away from youth and beauty. The predominant pressure on women comes from a widespread assumption that only the young are attractive. Many older women begin to believe this fallacy themselves. In addition, many adult children do not accept sexuality in their parents' lives. They define their parents in purely parental roles. These societal attitudes, coupled with adult children's negative attitudes about their parents' sexual intimacy, may be more important reasons why older adults are not sexually active than the biological changes they experience with aging.

Ageism is a systematic discrimination against people because they are old. The ageist perceives older people as rigid, senile, old-fashioned in their world view, useless and, therefore, a burden on society. Ageist attitudes are responsible for the idea that older people lack energy and are devoid of sexual feelings and are, therefore, not interested in sexual intimacy. Since sexuality tends to be equated with youthful standards of attractiveness, definitions of older people as asexual are heightened for older women and men with chronic illness, disability, and general loss of positive physical attributes.

Other attitudes and beliefs may be the result of misinformation such as the idea that sexual activity and drive do and should decline with old age. Unfortunately, the widely held attitude in our society that sexual interaction between older persons is socially unacceptable and even physically harmful may have negative consequences for older people. Surrounded by those with such beliefs and fearing laughter or criticism, many older people may unnecessarily withdraw from all forms of sexual expression long before they need to, thereby depriving themselves and often their partners of the energy and vitality inherent in sexuality.

In the novel *Love in the Time of Cholera*[1] Gabriel Garcia Marquez writes about a great unspoken theme in the youthful culture of North America: sexual intimacy between two old people. Without guilt or shame and in spite of her shocked middle-aged children who believed that "there was an age at which love began to be indecent," Fermina and Florentino "... exchanged unhurried kisses; they enjoyed the rapture of caresses." And she "accepted with pleasure when Florentino dared to explore her withered neck with his fingertips, her bosom armored in metal stays, her hips with their decaying bones, her thighs with their aging veins." This older couple embraced their love and did not back away: "They can all go to hell... if there is any advantage it is that there is no one left to give us orders."

While individuals ultimately decide what ethical system, if any, they choose to follow, society plays a strong role in determining which values are upheld and which are discouraged. Our values, experiences, families, peers, media, religion, law, and government all influence sexuality, gender roles, and sexual behaviors. The oldest-old, people aged 85+, grew up in times of restrictive guidelines regarding appropriate sexual behavior and taboos against other forms of sexual activity. Therefore, it is sometimes harder for this cohort of older adults to give themselves freely to sexual expression. They have difficulty overcoming guilt and shame in light of ingrained childhood teachings.

Religion shapes sexual values with "sacred" law that articulates a range of acceptable sexual behaviors and practices (who an individual can marry, the types of sexual expression allowed, the use of contraception, etc.). In the Judeo-Christian tradition of Western societies, the Old and New Testament prohibitions against sexuality in both its specific and general forms have proven to be immensely powerful forces. They have demanded and justified repression of sexual thought and conduct and have provided heavy burdens of guilt and shame. Explicit prohibitions can be found against nakedness, masturbation, and homosexuality.

In contrast to these Judeo-Christian prohibitions are the joyful, yet spiritual Hindu "verses of desire" found in the *Kama Sutra*.[2] This religiously oriented mythology/philosophy advocates a balance between spiritual, material, cultural, and sensual realms of life. Simply put, the central concept that should be noted is this: the individual must live his life with balance – a balance between Dharma (quest for spiritual and religious merit), Artha (quest for fortune and social standing), and Kama (quest for love and sensual pleasure). To put this in modern terms, a person does not ignore his inner self (his spiritual and emotional core), his social duties (such as to family, community, career), but neither does he ignore his sensuality and his need for love and sexual fulfillment. Rather he/she seeks to address all the facets of life in balanced measure. Therefore, Hindu mythology teaches that the souls of men and women could be elevated to a higher level of being through enlightened sexual activity.

Human sexuality is basically the same everywhere. However, every society imposes some form of control over the expression of love and sexuality between individuals. The social world in which today's elderly grew up would not have allowed them to examine what I described above. The current cohort of older adults grew up during a period when sexual behavior was not discussed, when encouragement of sexual feeling was suppressed, and when instruction in sex education was minimal. Even the most "liberated" knew little of the facts of life, and most held to strong superstitions. Therefore, open communication about sex and sexuality was totally inappropriate.

However, for future generations the misinformation and shamefulness associated with a discussion of sexually-charged issues was forever unmasked with the publication of the first of Alfred Kinsey's volumes, *Sexual Behavior in the Human Male*[3] in 1948 and followed in 1953 with the release of *Sexual Behavior of the Human Female.*[4] Kinsey's surveys of human sexuality produced a social explosion with the methodical dissection of Americans' sex life and correlated these trends with subjects' occupation, education, and church attendance in addition to other significant variables. Previously, Americans had to rely on pornography, older siblings and the family doctor for information about sex. The desire for better information and a natural curiosity about what the neighbors were doing in their bedrooms couched in the aura of dispassionate scientific respectability made the books overnight bestsellers. Kinsey had given the American public a legitimate reason to openly discuss sex – it was scientific!

Kinsey's interviews (approximately 18,000) represent a snapshot of some portion of America during the 1940s, not a statistically representative sample as many have criticized. Granting the flaws of the known sampling techniques of the time, the broad conclusions Kinsey drew from his data have withstood the test of time and it is those conclusions that ultimately changed the way Americans converse about and behave around the topic of sex. It is a tribute to Kinsey's ability as a researcher that the trends he recorded and the inferences drawn from his analysis are credible today.

Our ideas about old age are archaic, based on outdated models. The combined effect of the senior boom and the birth dearth in America has created a senior population who, with the gift of longevity and the added years it brings, will be redefining the style and purpose of those later years of life for themselves that include love and sex. We cannot anticipate the changes that will be brought about by population aging by looking backward because these concepts are unprecedented in human history. The rules of aging have been forever altered as the lifestyles and life cycles of the older population are continuously being reinvented. The concept of reinventing yourself postretirement is a groundbreaking one. It requires throwing away the negative stereotypes and myths of aging that have been accepted until now. If given the opportunity, the trick is to create a new life stage that provides meaning, structure, and purpose rather than acceptance, inflexibility, and withdrawal.

The Baby Boom generation can be defined by its place in history. All were born into post-World War II society, with its revolution in social values and customs. The world inhabited by this cohort can be characterized by greater sexual freedom, increased empowerment of women and minorities, and antiauthoritarianism which extends to all groups and professional bodies that challenge them. This cohort will be far more confident about being old – confidence derived from being part of the largest cohort in the history of human kind which has enjoyed huge strides in education and technology. This cohort will not tolerate ageism and will, therefore, refuse to be harassed or intimidated in any of its pursuits.

"He's rather good at retrieving my thong."

Sexual interest, capacities, and functions change with age. For the most part, like many biological and psychological functions, these dimensions of sexuality decline with increasing age. These changes need to be viewed as part of the normal aging process; it does not mean that older men and women in reasonably good health should not be able to have an active and satisfying sex life. Older people desire closeness and touching that is so much a part of our humanness despite the possibility of decreases in levels of arousal and a lessening in intensity.

Men do not generally lose their capacity to have erections and ejaculations as they age. However, any changes that occur in sexual physiology of an aging male relevant to erectile function and ejaculation need not have any functional impact on the subjective enjoyment of the sexual encounter. Knowledge that these changes are not dysfunctional and assistance with the adjustment of sexual practices may be crucial in preventing dysfunction due to performance anxiety. The patterns of sexual activity of healthy men as they grow older tend to reflect earlier patterns in their lives, although with a slower physical response associated with aging. Physical or psychological difficulties that may occur are usually treatable.

The medical profession has long debated the existence of male menopause. There is certainly no physical "menopause" or climacteric in men that is parallel to that in women because hormone loss in men does not occur abruptly. Decreases in the male hormone testosterone take place very gradually over time.

Some normal **changes that occur as men get older** include:

- Decreased production of testosterone which stabilizes around age 60
- Size and firmness of the testicles may be reduced because of testosterone stabilizing
- Reduction in sperm count
- Erection may be delayed and/or may not be as firm as when younger
- Longer time before ejaculation
- Orgasm is shorter than when younger
- Time between orgasms can take anywhere from 12 to 24 hours
- Men who remain sexually active in their youth and middle years tend to have fewer issues with continued sexual satisfaction as they get older
- Remember that masturbation is sex, and that while a man may not have a sex partner, he can continue to be a sexual person through self-loving

Many men find that after spending a lifetime working towards the goals of family and peers, the result is unsatisfactory. There is sometimes a *mid-life crisis* when they are in their forties-fifties and its occurrence results from psychological factors. At this time, job-related stability has usually been achieved and the social and economic struggles that were once a large part of life are now less stressful. For some men, this new found stability may signify an end to vitality or youth. The awareness that a life change has taken place can sometimes trigger a crisis. In addition, along with the physical signs of aging comes a realization of our own mortality. Therefore, a man's mid-life crisis may signal the need for a psychosocial adjustment and once this has been addressed, any issues related to his sexual life may also be put in its proper perspective.

Except for the effects of estrogen loss after menopause, the normal physical changes that accompany aging appear to interfere very little with a woman's sexual ability. Although women continue to be sexual throughout their lives, there are some changes that may accompany their sexual response as they age. Illness, disability, and medications may affect sexual interest and performance, but much of the impact appears to be psychological, based upon societal myths associated with women's sexuality as they age, personal preferences, or lack of a partner.

Some physical **changes in the female as she gets older** include:

- Menopause occurs after the age of 45-50. With the elimination of pregnancy as an issue, many women find sexual desire to increase
- The expansive ability of the vagina is diminished during sexual arousal
- Lubrication begins slower and the amount is less
- Sensitivity in the clitoris and nipples remain the same as when younger
- Sexual tension that mounts right before orgasm is less dramatic
- Phase after orgasm occurs more rapidly for the post-menopausal woman, but she is still capable of achieving multiple orgasms as in her earlier years

For both men and women the middle years can be seen as either a cup half empty or a cup half-full. An important aspect of adjustment to getting older is the ability to derive meaning from experiences and the realization that life has a purpose. When people are capable of transforming negative events into opportunities, the result is personal growth and life satisfaction. When people think about the good things that have happened in the first half of their lives, it should be exciting to imagine that every bit as much can happen in the second half.

One of the most significant factors influencing sexual behavior among older people is the large disparity between the number of men and women. A profound emotional and sexual situation facing older women revolves around the possibility of finding themselves alone – widowed, divorced, separated, or single as they grow older. Among people age 65 and over, there are almost one and half times as many women as men; there are not enough men to go around. It is not always possible for an older woman to have a sexual partner. Husbands die or move on to younger women and many women face the prospect of being either self-sexual or non-sexual.

The effect of the Feminist Movement coupled with the sheer number of well educated confident women who are socialized to the workplace will greatly influence their lives as they age. They will feel far freer than today's older adults to enter nontraditional intimate relationships – an advantage for women where the risk of isolation in late life is greater. The media, with its emphasis on young, reproductive women, often denies women the ability to picture themselves as sexually deserving. From card shops to policy decisions, and from media images to popular culture, older women have been devalued. However, advances in treating male dysfunction has led to a new focus on the sexuality of older women, underscored by a recognition that, because of their longer lives, older women represent an untapped larger pharmaceutical consumer group than men. The male oriented sexual research is giving way to equal curiosity about older women and their needs for sexual expression.

Sexual expression is generally perceived as being reserved for the young while it is inherent to one's human condition. Lust in old age is deemed unseemly; the fires of passion should either burn out or be screened because the image of aging flesh enmeshed in lustful sexual acts remains for many a repellent one. As we grow old and society counts us out of the game of life, if we do not resist society's views, we can learn to hate ourselves. Many older persons believe they have become ugly and undesirable and begin to hate the way they look as a result of the aging process. They make frantic attempts to appear young and become depressed at the futility of the efforts to alter their physical appearance. When older people give up on themselves and their sexuality they give up on sensual pleasure, physical intimacy, and heightened self-worth. For as Longfellow's poem "Morituri Salutamus" reminds us, "... nothing is too late/Till the tired heart shall cease to palpitate."[7]

WOMAN PINCHING MAN'S BOTTOM AHEAD

Grizelda

More and more studies are confirming what many older Americans already know, age does not necessarily impact the desire for sex. There are some sexual issues that are unique to older people. However, if sexuality has not been a constant in one's life, being older does not have to be a deterrent. If sexuality has been a constant throughout life, the biological changes associated with aging are less pronounced and sexuality is usually less affected. One can rediscover, or discover for the first time, the joy of being a sexual person.

Sexuality is as normal and natural in old age as it is in early adulthood. While we see many examples in the media of young love, we seldom see examples of older people enjoying sex. Sleeping in the same bed locked in an embrace, holding hands, kissing, gazing into one another's eyes, giving or receiving a massage, or even holding hands in a dark movie theater can be as exciting and stimulating as sexual intercourse or oral sex. It is really up to the individual couple to define for themselves what they mean by sexuality. As we age, we often redefine what we mean by sex, not necessarily because of an inability to perform certain activities, but more because we have a better understanding of what it means to each of us.

In 1998, the National Council on Aging[9] interviewed 1300 adults over 60 and surveyed their sexual activities. The results indicate that sexual activity plays an important role in relationships among older men and women. Of these respondents, 79% of men and 66% of women said that sex was an important component of their relationship with their partner. Seventy-four percent of the sexually active men and 70% of the sexually active women reported being as satisfied as or even more satisfied with their sexual lives than they were in their 40's. Recent studies show that sexuality and sex do not come to a screeching halt. Rather, more than a quarter of Americans 75 or older have sex at least once a week according to Modern Maturity and AARP. Seventy-one percent of men in their sixties report having sex once a month or more and 51% of women in their sixties report having sex once a month or more according to the Minneapolis Star Tribune.

The Pfizer Global Study of Sexual Attitudes and Behaviors[10] (2002) is the first contemporaneous global survey to study behaviors, attitudes, beliefs and satisfaction with relationships. The study reported the importance of sex and intimacy in men and women ages 40-80 across 29 countries. In this survey of more than 27,000 respondents, 83% of men and 63% women said that sex was very or at least moderately important in their lives. In response to a question on frequency of sexual activity within the past year, 57% men and 51% women answered at least 1-6 times per week. These results suggest that older people are interested and desire sexual intimacy. It is also likely that when they are sexually abstinent, it is because they have no available partner or because of health problems. In *The Joy of Sex*[11] (1974), Alex Comfort wrote:

> **The only thing age has to do with sex performance is that the longer you love, the more you learn. Young people (and some older ones) are firmly convinced that no one over fifty makes love, and it would be pretty obscene if they did. Ours isn't the**

first generation to know otherwise, but probably the first one which hasn't been brainwashed into being ashamed to admit it!

Love and a sexual turn-on do not occur just because of outer beauty. In an older couple, years of loving one another are a turn-on in itself. For older people, emotional security, being able to depend upon and trust one another, mutual respect and admiration and the ability to communicate honestly are the keys to happy love relationships in later life. The last but not least important factor is sexual intimacy. Sexuality for older adults becomes an affirmation of a lifetime of shared experiences and memories; it is a way of expressing love. Aren't these the same ingredients valued at any age? Is the nature of a new love in late life different from a love relationship shared over fifty years? Older couples appear to have more tolerance and patience. Older adults simply accept one another.

When the Old Folks Make Love

When the old folks make love,
they cry out softly in the dark,
They kiss each other's eyes and shoulders,
laugh and sleep, dream and wake
and murmur, "dearest."
Their eyelids flutter like gauze curtains,
They breathe into each other's mouths, softly,
She says, "I dreamed the children
were small again in our old house."
He says."I dreamed of fly fishing."

When the old folks make love,
They frame each other's faces,
with their hands,
like a favorite photograph.
They touch each other's lips and cheeks,

they melt together, not
with the raging, aching burst of summer,
but with a deep, slow sob
like the sound of a temple bell
coming up from Atlantis.

When the old folks make love
their bodies fit together like
pieces of a puzzle.
They sigh together in one single sigh.
One says, "This is so good."
The other smiles in the dark.

When the old folks make love,
they start in the kitchen
with coffee and The Times,
end up in bed
rubbing their feet together,
pulling each other's ears.
They whisper, "beloved,"
and "dear little face,"
and sometimes fall out
of bed, laughing.

When the old folks make love,
they tell each other stories
of a thousand nights and one
that they loved and fought
and wept and sulked
and went to bed angry,
knowing you're not supposed to,
lived silently for days

and only made up because
they bumped into each other
accidentally, in this bed.

When the old folks make love,
each makes a space
for the other to enter freely.
They write, "I love you,"
on each other's skin
again and again
like a poem.[12]

—Niki Nymark, 2002

Women's mid-life journey
If not now, then when...?

Menopause is a commencement, a beginning. The women we were as we began menopause are different people than the ones we were when we lived through the "dramas" of budding sexuality, childbearing and mothering, fostering new careers, losses and health challenges, and perhaps positive transformations. We have gained immeasurable wisdom in the march through life's changing seasons.

"To everything there is a season and a time and a purpose under heaven. A time to be born and a time to die... " (Book of Ecclesiastes) and what happens in between those two fixed points is in some ways culturally and biologically predictable. There is a lot in the seasons of women's lives for which they alone are responsible. How they negotiate the seasons and how they reach out to others along the way is what makes a life challenging and worth living.

Just as in nature, women grow; they have their seasons and their reasons. Menopause provides a biological demarcation of a gradual process, not a signal that the end of sexuality or vitality is approaching. Menopause in women is an observable series of events resulting in loss of reproductive capacity, whereas men may continue their reproductive abilities well into old age. Men may experience some reduction in testosterone levels, which diminishes sex drive, but this is not a universal phenomenon. Menopause propels women to explore if they have a purpose under heaven or anywhere else.

Thomas Mann's *The Black* Swan[1] (1954) is set in 1920s Germany and is written from the point of view of a middle-aged woman, Rosalie, who while reacting to the physical changes of menopause falls in love with her son's tutor. However, she misreads her own physiological state. She deludes herself into thinking that she is pregnant when in fact her bloating stomach is a symptom of her eventual death from ovarian cancer.

Mann's novella is an exploration of what a woman who can no longer bear a child and who is aging thinks she has to offer a younger man. The new introduction to the book places this novella in the context of contemporary feminist and literary concerns bringing it to the attention of a new generation of readers. Thomas Whitman has turned this drama into a chamber opera that was performed for the first time at Swarthmore College in 2001.

If women were to treat their menopausal bodies with the same care and level of nurturance that they reserve for the pregnant or nursing woman, this amazing time would translate into another loving season in the cycle of their existence. Women in the United States often receive the message that one of the most important times of change, the menopause, is terrible. The drug companies, male physicians, and most of all the advertising media, have given women the message that this change is a time to be dreaded, avoided, and postponed. Some of the physical discomforts are exacerbated by our culture's beliefs that aging is not a natural phenomenon but a failure to remain young. It is hard to maintain self-worth when the society in which we live tells us we are past our prime. However, the sheer number of women in or anticipating menopause may at last confer normalcy on this predictable journey.

Meaning Menopause

My gynecologist calls it
ovarian failure.
I didn't make this up,
nor did he. He learned it
in medical school,
reads it in journals,

says it casually
to his colleagues,
who say it back to him.
Every day he flunks
his patients with it
and they take it on the chin,
but when he serves it
up to me, something snaps.
How funny he looks,
clenching a speculum
in his gloved hand,
trying to calm me
while I shriek like a fury
and challenge him
to evict me in my paper gown.
His eyes travel furtively
to his watch as he recalls
his waiting room,
now full to overflowing
with women whose
ovaries are failing
even as they turn the pages
of their magazines. Too bad,
I am going to lie right here,
howling and kicking my feet
on the stirrups
until he recants – this man
so certain of his truth,
whose testicles
know nothing but success. [2]

—*Dori Appel 1991*

Although menopause is a universal feminine journey, each woman is idiosyncratic in her experience with it. The waves each chooses to ride are hers and hers alone. Some women have terrible hot flashes and night sweats; some go through a profound period of self-discovery, others a sense of loss, anxiety, and depression; some women cannot get through it without hormone replacement while others hardly notice its passage. Ultimately, it is a choice each woman must make to accept the time of life she is living.

Although sometimes a difficult and demanding passage of adulthood, menopause can also be a time of increased strength and growth. Women emerge from menopause not only older, but also changed in some way. In *Number Our Days* [3](1978), the late anthropologist Barbara Myerhoff borrowed from the Psalmists who urged "… teach us to number our days that we may get a heart of wisdom." (p.xvii). What is a heart of wisdom? This question reflects concerns about identity, the self, and the good life. They are evaluative questions and provide us with the possibility to make choices. Each stage of our life brings its own lessons and joys, as we take the soil of whom we are and plant the seeds of the woman we are yet to become.

The nature of the life's course bears little resemblance to the experience of prior generations. Ken Dychtwald, author of *Age Wave* [4] (1988) described the linear life plan as based directly on the biological and social requirements of the short length of life in earlier times. The various activities of life were performed on time, and in sequence. Most of life's periods of growth took place in the first half of life, while the second half was generally characterized by decline.

Many Baby Boomers followed traditional patterns of marriage, employment, and childbearing while the timing of life events for other Baby Boomers has varied widely. The latter group has been instrumental in the dissolution of the traditional linear life plan. In its place, they have opted for a much more flexible arrangement, the "cyclic life plan." Longer life has eliminated the rigid correlations between age and the various roles and activities and challenges of adult life. Time spent in education has pushed back the timing of childbearing so that women, not just men, can extend the timing of child rearing well into the mature decades of life. Whereas education has been primarily geared to preparing for lifetime careers, we are now coming to think of learning as an ongoing, lifelong process. With the cyclic life plan, most people will have more years of adult life after the children have grown and have left home than they had when they were raising them.

The *Pirke Avot* is a portion of the Talmud that is reserved for stories and maxims, the ethical teachings of the rabbis who lived in the period from about 300B.C. to 200A.D. The *Pirke Avot* records that: "Hillel used to ask: 'If I am not for myself, who will be for me'"? [5] *The Second Sex*[6] by Simone de Beauvoir (1953) powerfully showed how women's second-class status was a social invention. If women could be socialized to believe they were second, they could also be made to believe they were first or equal to men. De Beauvoir's theory that women are made, not born, galvanized a whole generation of women and made them eager to adjust and/or transform their roles, status, and aspirations. As said by Germaine Greer, the Australian feminist writer in *The Change: Women, Aging and the Menopause:* "The climacteric marks the end of apologizing. The chrysalis of conditioning has once for all to break and the female woman finally to emerge."[7] At age 65, Laura Ingalls Wilder published *Little House in the Big Woods,* the first of her eight-volume "Little House" series. At 93, Lillian Gish starred in the film "The Whales of August," 72 years after appearing in the landmark film, "The Birth of a Nation."

Through literature, the arts, and popular culture, people can question the negative stereotypes that they encounter while also using these media to construct images that are more positive. Inspiring feature films and thought-provoking documentaries are useful and entertaining art forms to illustrate natural and universal human joys and frailties. *Antonia's Line*[8] won an Academy Award for best foreign film in 1995. The film portrays a family chronicle, following not the male line, but the female. This movie compares to *Like Water for Chocolate*[9] as they are both told in flashback by a contemporary woman in the case of the Mexican film by a great grand niece, and in the case of *Antonia's Line* by Antonia's great granddaughter. Both movies present feminist and humanist values that resist being sentimental but rather filled with joys and tragedies and a sense of life progressing in its own organic cycles both in nature and in the communities and families inspired by the stories.

Some women may come to learn that their strength lies not in their youth or in their ability to bear children and nurture their families but in their own personal power. Many women find in later life that what they thought was going to make them happy no longer does. One may have enjoyed law school and the first few years in practice. However, the thought of practicing law for the rest of one's life may not be very fulfilling. This is a time when a woman shines a light on her accomplishments and sets an agenda for the second half of life. Depending upon the outcome of her evaluation, there may or may not be major changes.

As the female hormones decline, the masculine hormones become more potent. Male hormones increase libido and assertion in both genders. Clinical experts have described the dramatically altered balance between female and male hormones due to menopause. In a pre-menopausal woman, the ratio of testosterone to estrogen is roughly two to one; in a postmenopausal woman the ratio is roughly twenty to one. This provides a biological basis that would explain in part why postmenopausal women attest to greater assertiveness cross-culturally. Since aggressiveness is rooted in the male hormone testosterone and found in elevated levels in men, it may follow that postmenopausal women fired up with relatively higher levels of testosterone rise in rank and power in political, religious, economic, and community life.

For many women, menopause signals an increase in stronger emotional responses; women may express emotions more directly, become more assertive, and more sexual. Beyond the physical changes in our bodies, there are other weighty changes in our interests, focus, and aspirations. Menopause is about new beginnings in the second half of life. It is a time to be, to do, and to reflect. Rather than detracting from ourselves with judgments about what we could have done and who we could have become, it is more rewarding if we redirect our energy from good enough to better on any level and in any direction of our choice. In Doris Lessing's book, *The Golden Notebook* (1962)[10] the protagonist is a writer trying to write a novel about contemporary women but she is blocked. She is seeking a way of integrating the disparate parts of her life. The journey of Lessing's book is a woman's struggle to harmonize all her passions.

Women past the stormy hormonal adjustments have a more stable physiology, freeing the emotions from the hormonal roller coaster that has disturbed them. Margaret Mead's famous observation that there is no force on earth equal to that of women with post-menopausal zest begins the reframing of aging which is demanded of this time. Menopausal women in America today have longer life expectancy than any previous generation. Women have always had the energy to do more than their culture or designated social roles permitted. Baby Boomers are leading the way for pre-menopausal women to follow who may be less encumbered by the baggage of doing it the way "it's always been done." It is not even possible to follow the courses laid out by previous generations of women. It is especially true for women whose lives no longer need be dominated by the rhythms of procreation and the dependences that these created, but who must still balance the conflicting demands in their lives.

What are they planning to do with these bonus years; how will they remain productive, able to cope while realizing their dreams? They may learn to be courageous adult women who take responsibility for their own needs and growth. For some women, spending time and money to reverse or postpone the natural aging process may fulfill a need. However, they may realize that they are missing the beauty found in less feverish living. In addition, while aging is not for sissies, if we are lucky, it is better than the alternative. If women go with the tide instead of raging against it, they can continue to be creative, joyful and productive to the end of their days. We need to embrace the strong role models of menopausal and postmenopausal women as they begin to reject the old images of menopause. Women need to listen to their bodies and psyche, follow their creative instincts and use them fully to live all the stages of their life.

The Internet has opened up a plethora of information in almost unlimited areas to titillate our interest. One site (http://www.txc.net.au/-mapie/midlifecrisisfor women.htm) provides a satirical take-off on women's midlife crisis. If you find the site humorous, crack yourself up and share it with your friends. If it shocks and scares you to the point that you realistically contemplate plastic surgery, then that is okay, too. Again, because this chapter is devoted to challenges and choices at mid-life, please follow or disavow the message of the Internet site – it is your choice.

In *Pirke Avot* [5] Hillel continues by asking: "… if I am for myself alone, what am I?" If we are for ourselves alone, we overlook and neglect the needs and aspirations of others. Most women will not choose to teach but all will teach – in the workplace, in the community, in the family. Others have much to gain from what women have learned in their lives. Women can nurture in others what their life experiences have encouraged them to develop for themselves. As women leave reproductive mothering, they actually enter into a phase of even greater nurturance of the larger community. They can serve their communities not only in primary careers but also through involvement with voluntary organizations. Each woman has the life experiences to see problems in a new light, to think them through again, and provide more holistic solutions. Women who consider themselves successful in their evolving roles continue to build lasting structures of relationships and accomplishments, believe that one has influence over the course of life events, and believe that change can be a stimulus for growth on a personal as well as community level.

Finally, Hillel asks "… and if not now, when?"[5] In interpreting the last of Hillel's questions, it may very well remind us that we may never get the same opportunity twice. Getting older means that there is a limit to our time, so who is going to bother with stuff that does not mean much to us? At the same time, menopause reminds us of our mortality so we have a sense of urgency to get on with those things that we have always wanted to do but have kept putting off because of the demands of marriage, childbearing and work. The best we can do, at this moment in time, is to make the smartest personal choices available to us.

Women need to recognize that many options are available; many approaches and styles may be adapted to find individual solutions that fit. Giving and sharing information and experiences, in a way that can be understood, allows each woman personal choices. Although women cannot know how menopause will affect them, they can prepare for it by informing themselves, listening to those who have been there, and then taking the responsibility of showing younger women how healthy and powerful the later years can be.

If nature has prolonged women's lives 25-40 years beyond menopause, it is important to create/discover their purpose in the bigger picture and to use their living and evolving wisdom for the good of themselves and with whom they share life. Older women have a responsibility to take on with pride that of showing younger women how healthy and powerful the later years are. They need to follow their instincts and learn, and, in turn, teach. Rabbi Tarfon, a second century scholar reminds us: "You are not required to complete the work, but neither are you free to desist from it."[12]

Marriage: Growing older together

"And they lived happily ever after... What was their marriage like? As the years passed, did the prince undergo a mid-life crisis and the princess a hysterectomy? Did she decide to color her golden hair and he to take up jogging along the palace walls?

OR

Did she want no one but him? And did they spend their days walking hand in hand in the palace gardens waiting for sunset?"[1]

Khalil Gibran's passage "On Marriage" from *The Prophet* [2] describes that the above alternative scenarios are perhaps two parts of the same evolving marriage:

> *Give your hearts, but not into each other's keeping.*
> *For only the hand of Life can contain your hearts.*
> *And stand together, yet not too near together,*
> *For the pillars of the temple stand apart,*
> *And the oak tree and the cypress*
> *Grow not in each other's shadow.*

Most older couples today have grown old together. Because more people are living longer, their marriages have a chance to live longer, too. Despite the lack of partners for many older women, high marriage and remarriage rates mean that older couples are very prevalent even among older people. The couple relationship tends to be the focal point in married people's lives. As life expectancy increases, so does the average number of years a couple can expect to live together after their children leave home.

Whereas wedding ceremonies throughout history have served to unite families and accumulate wealth and influence, today love rather than family or power is the motivating force behind most marriages. As a young couple stand at the altar today they can look forward to spending the next half century or more together. *The Notebook* (2004)[3], a film based on the novel by Nicholas Sparks, is a romantic love story exemplifying the marriage vow to love your spouse "in sickness and in health, 'till death do us part.'" Unlike most cinema love stories, this one takes us beyond the mere beginning of a true love and shows us the way it ends. The story can easily resonate with older couples who have been together for many years. It may also inspire the current cohorts of younger people to affirm, value, and celebrate the commitment to marriage.

At the turn of the century, more than half of all marriages were interrupted by the death of one spouse, usually the husband, before the last child left home. Today, most married couples look forward to the post parenting years as opportunities for increased closeness and companionship. Older couples are often less lonely and financially more stable than older single persons. The couple relationship is a source of great comfort and support as well as the focal point of everyday life especially with the departure of adult children. AND, for better or for worse, when retirement from work increases the amount of contact between them.

About His Retirement

He's pointing out where I left some dust on the baseboards.
He's watching out for which foods I am letting go bad.
He's giving me guidance on how to water the houseplants.
He says that I ought to be glad. I am not glad.

He's nudging me when I fail to floss after mealtime.
He's alerting me when I gain even half a pound.
He's pestering me to straighten my spine and stop slouching

Whenever he's around. He is always around.

He's starting conversations with me when I'm reading.
He's chiming in when I talk with my friends on the phone.
He's coming with me when I shop at the supermarket
So I won't have to shop alone. I like alone.

He's sitting beside me while I'm tweezing my eyebrows.
He's standing beside me while I'm blow-drying my hair.
He's sharing those moments when I am clipping my toenails.
You want my opinion? He's overdoing share.

He's keeping track of how I am spending each second.
He also keeps track of how much I spend on my clothes.
Before he retired I told him he must find a hobby.
Now he's retired. And guess who's the hobby he chose?[4]

—Judith Viorst 2000

Finnegan Alford-Cooper (1998) [5] surveyed over 500 couples who had been married 50 years of more. She reported that there were high degrees of compatibility among these spouses; they confided in their spouse; and, eighty percent felt that their spouse understood them and was their best friend. More often than not, a strong love relationship has a deep abiding friendship at its core.

Non-Stop

Someone asked me
To name the time
Our friendship stopped
And love began.

Oh, my darling,
That's the secret.
Our friendship
Never stopped. [6]

—*Lois Wyse 1967*

Love is friendship with a few added components.*Enjoyment* – friends enjoy each other's company most of the time; friends accept one another and do not try to change the other person. *Trust* – friends assume that they will act in one another's best interest. *Commitment* – is the glue that holds a relationship together. *We-ness* – refers to the degree that a couple participates in their relationship as a team rather than as two separate people; they focus mostly on their shared relationship and history and move towards their future together.

I Love How You Love Me[7]

I love how your eyes close whenever you kiss me
And when I'm away from you I love how you miss me
I love the way you always treat me tenderly
But, darling, most of all I love how you love me
(love how you love me)

I love how your heart beats whenever I hold you
I love how you think of me without being told to
I love the way your touch is always heavenly
But, darling, most of all I love how you love me
(love how you love me)

I love how your eyes close whenever you kiss me
And when I'm away from you I love how you miss me
I love the way your touch is always heavenly

But, darling, most of all I love how you love me
(love how you love me)

I love how you hug me (love how you hug me)
I love how you squeeze me, tease me, please me
Love—how you love me
I love how you love me

—*Bobby Vinton*

Thank you for the passion, the friendship, and the shared history...

Older couples are survivors that reflect the aging of our society whose unprecedented number are marching towards Golden Pond together. More significantly, since they have had few role models, they are explorers mapping out new territory on what it is like to grow old in America today as individuals and as a couple. If one focuses on the paradoxes of old age, he/she will find painful dilemmas on one side balanced by the challenges and opportunities on the other and how these impact on each person in the partnership and on the couple.

Old age is a time of radical change and it has many faces. It comes in all shapes and sizes, strengths and weaknesses, personalities and behavior patterns. However, how people weather the changes and often multiple losses in old age depends upon their own personality, their individual coping mechanisms and how they view themselves and their partners. The starring roles in this chapter are portrayed by couples. However, how each of the partners interprets his/her own personal aging is a very individual process. The sociologist Jessie Bernard has described every marriage as really two marriages - his marriage and her marriage with the possibility of even a third marriage, "our marriage", and the one the couple jointly present to the outside world and even to one another. Each side would tell a very different story about the same relationship and each one would likely interpret late life according to his/her personal timetable and individual experiences and emotions.[1]

China (2003)[8] is a thoughtful, quietly moving drama about an older married African American couple, Rudolph and Evelyn Jackson, whose lives radically change when Rudolph suddenly decides to take up martial arts. Evelyn fears that her old Rudolph will hasten his demise attempting this foolishness but what happens at his match rekindles Evelyn's love for her man. It reminds us, too, of the endless adventures in a long and loving marriage and life.

Half-Squeezed

Somewhere in the
Half-squeezed tube of toothpaste,
In the comb of mine
You use,
In the TV shows we lie and watch...
Somewhere in all of this
We sink our roots.

We draw our strength
In such strange ways.
We build our life
On toothpaste, combs, and
Television shows with highly predictable
endings.[9]

—Lois Wyse 1967

When one vows at the onset of a marriage to live together "for better, for worse," one anticipates little of the "for worse." Yet losses in late life are painful but inevitable. The loss of close relatives and friends is the price we pay for outliving our loved ones. Other losses may include loss of role and status, financial security, health and independence. These are all a part of marriage, especially in the later years. Given the scope of negative changes, what possible positive opportunities can one look forward to? Not having to work yet having a reasonable income is a major compensation for many people. Many late-lifers look forward to fewer parental responsibilities, more leisure time, or even the prospect of embarking on new careers. In addition, one is particularly grateful for the support and love of a lifelong partner – someone who remembers you as you once were and who continues to care for you as you are now. This bond is an irreplaceable attachment to the person who has shared your history with you.

The current cohort of older adult women (65-85+ or the Baby Boomers anticipating retirement) married at a significantly younger age than many women do now. Most of these women grew up before the sexual revolution. One can argue about whether the cultural changes seen since then have been beneficial or harmful to society, but that argument is beside the point. Many women learned how to live with another person, how to adjust and change in an intimate relationship with a spouse. Some were able to build mutually nourishing long-term marriages; some were not so fortunate. Every marriage is a story unto itself.

Despite all the variations in the timetables of the aging process, there is one certainty: late life is a stage that couples will share more closely than any other period. The individual feelings both partners have about growing old affects their relationship, and vice versa: their relationship affects how they feel about growing old. Two people may be in complete disagreement about their own personal aging, but when each one is able to counteract the other's fears and weaknesses with reassurance and understanding, both become stronger in the process. This support, however, depends largely on the shared biography of the couple and how it developed throughout their marriage. This support will also depend upon the couple's ability and willingness to readjust their relationship, revise long-standing negative patterns, and shift priorities to make them adapt better to late life. When individuals have taken the time to learn to recognize their partner's emotional needs and how to satisfy them, then their relationship can probably withstand most dilemmas.

Although there is lack of information of sexual intimacy in the lives of older couples, the information that does exist suggests that marriages in which sexual behavior has not noticeably changed tends to be happier than marriages in which there has been a marked decline in sexual behavior. As a group, older lovers value emotional security above all: being able to depend and trust one another. They value respect, admiration, and the ability to communicate with each other. Working, playing and sharing sexual intimacy are also part of this "love connection."

As Time Goes By[10] the British television movie series, televised by PBS (1992-2005), actively challenged the cultural assumptions that along with age comes a disinterest in sex and intimacy between older couples. The series provided a frank discussion of the emotional and physical needs of the elderly which do not disappear when a person has passed some arbitrary chronological milestone. It described what most of us want: love and affection, whether it takes the form of hand-holding, cuddling, or sexual intercourse.

However, as we grow older, for some spouses, fear of failure, or "performance anxiety," plays an important role in the tendency of some husbands to withdraw from sexual activity. A wife may sometimes lack the insight or fear taking the initiative in addressing this problem and mistakenly feel rejected by her husband's apparent lack of interest in sex.

Counseling sometimes alleviates these issues but older couples, even if they think this issue is important, are reluctant to seek out counseling.

Many older couples report that they are sexually active and have experienced an increase in the spontaneity of sexual expression since their children have left the nest and they now have more unhurried quality time to express their sexual desire. Most report enjoying sex because it gives each partner feelings of desirability, completion and of being loved and loving. Sex is a powerful expression of intimacy, and its continuation into later life is important for the vast majority of older couples. The increase in marital satisfaction is the result of enhanced intimacy and a sense of belonging. It is these factors that unite the couple in an increasingly greater appreciation and acceptance of one another. Finally, the availability of a spouse to provide care giving when needed enhances older people's sense of safety, security, and encourages interdependence.

Older couples consciously make time for sex. The idea that the best sex is spontaneous is a myth. Most long-term couples plan their sexual experiences. For these couples, the mind leads the body more than the body leads the mind. McCarthy[11] has written that healthy, mutually pleasuring sex really helps strengthen the bond between couples. A study by Helen Fisher[12] revealed the unsurprising result that the more often a person has sex, the happier he or she is. This could be because people who have sex often are more likely to be healthy and enjoying a good relationship. It could also be because sex exercises the muscles and the respiratory system; gets the circulatory system moving, which gives the skin a gorgeous glow, and according to Fisher's research, triggers the brain circuitry for romantic love and attachment. Why do older couples continue to indulge in intimate sex? ***BECAUSE IT'S GREAT FUN***. It is the most powerful way to demonstrate love for ourselves and for someone else. When we open ourselves to the experience completely, we become intimate with the world in a way that's otherwise inaccessible.

A Chinese proverb states, "Married couples who love each other tell each other a thousand things without talking." Researchers estimate that approximately 70% of all communication is nonverbal. Many essential messages are transmitted through attitude, facial expressions, and body language – as well as through words that are left unsaid.

Partners need to be able to "read" one another's moods, attitudes, gestures and actions as well as the nonverbal messages that they receive or send to one another.

Today's older couples, in contrast to earlier ones who were members of two- and three-generation families, may belong to four-or five-generation families. The increased number of surviving generations has been offset by the dwindling number of people in each generation. This vertical structure is called the "beanpole" family. They may be sharing fifty or more years with children and often twenty-five years or more with grandchildren in which they can establish strong family bonds. With life expectancy on the rise, the fastest-growing segment of the population is the one 85 and older; less than a century ago life expectancy was less than 50 years. Therefore, more couples will retire with one or both of their parents still alive. As a result of this demographic change, many aging couples can connect with their own aging parents, their children, and even glimpse the future through their grown grandchildren.

Emphasis on the family arises from both the family's centrality in providing social care and its primacy in the lives of the elderly. Assistance tends to be based on a system of mutual reciprocity. In the case of family, such reciprocity stretches over the life cycle; the role of informal supports in providing affective, emotional support is often crucial and can be as important as the provision of instrumental support.

Older couples turn to their children not only for help in times of trouble but for pleasure and companionship. Many older couples, enjoying greater financial security than their own parents and grandparents did in the past, are willing and able to help their children financially while grown children reciprocate in kind whenever parents are ill or in need of instrumental assistance.

Today, in light of the varying family patterns, older couples who had expected freedom as they age often find themselves tied down, supporting children through professional studies and career changes. Now many aging parents are expected to be ready to nurse grown children through broken romances, illnesses, job disappointments, financial reversals, etc. When elderly parents are in failing health, the support and care their children are able and willing to give may become critical. Studies have shown that the most likely caregiver for a disabled wife is her husband, and vice versa. But next in line as caregivers are the couple's children. A mutual process of give-and-take characterizes the relationship between generations in the "beanpole" family.

Older couples may consider themselves lucky to be alive now if they consider that their marriage, just one hundred years ago, would have ended at middle age because of the death of one spouse. Now that marriage often continues for decades, they can grow old with a collection of relatives from every level of the "beanpole" family. However, couples who view the upward swing of life expectancy as the worst of times can point to any number of degenerating physical or mental diseases that occur most frequently in people over eighty-five; they may find themselves or their loved ones ill and dependent. Again, their perspective will be created by their own personal physical and mental coping mechanisms and the emotional and instrumental support they receive from one another and their families.

Retirement may contribute to marital satisfaction by reducing other commitments, role conflicts, and time constraints. It will also increase opportunities for companionship.[13] When daily life was crowded with work, household demands, children, and family responsibilities, couples had little time to spend with one another. If their lives are to continue to be satisfying as they retire, men and women need to work out patterns that complement their personalities and needs. Couples need to adjust their relationships according to each partner's needs and limits.

Yet couples who are determined to take control and nurture their relationship as they retire need to seek answers to questions not only limited to income, but to other conditions that can jeopardize the quality of their lives. They must create a dialogue that will consider housing choices, where to live; health care provision, medical and supportive help; decisions about death and dying; and, the very real possibility that one partner may have to function alone. However, once couples begin talking about these issues they may find that much more than health and wealth is involved here. They may realize that each of them may have some strong emotions and/or opinions about retirement issues that influence the personal relationship and any future plans. There may be some problems when couples disagree on how to spend money or how *not* to spend it.

Many husbands among today's cohort of elderly who were sole household breadwinners rarely consulted their wives about finances and future financial security. Wives were often willing to leave these decisions to their husbands assuming that their joint finances and hers were she to become widowed, would be assured. Too many women have lived to discover after widowhood or divorce how wrong their too-trusting assumptions had been. There are all too many stories of recently widowed women whose husbands made no provisions for them in their pension plan and they were left with little more than Social Security.

Women who face widowhood with financial security may also feel helpless because willingly or not they have remained ignorant about financial matters. Since demographics reveal that wives outlive their spouses by almost seven years, it is prudent that each partner be informed of, if not closely involved with, the overall financial picture.

"And do you, Grant, take Martha as your lawful wedded wife? Do you promise to love and honor her and *to obey the rules of good health*?" [1] This vow may not be in the traditional wedding ceremony, but in today's health conscious environment, it might as well be. "In sickness and in health" is one of the marriage vows and more often than not couples care for one another during serious but short-term illness and partial disability. However, in the later years, caring sometimes becomes the burden of long-term care giving that goes on until the death or institutionalization of the partner. Steps toward health promotion, such as improved diet or increased exercise can reduce the likelihood of illness and thus increase quantity and quality of life. Therefore, the buzz word today is prevention.

Many older people, having the time and inclination to take care of their bodies, are getting serious about physical fitness and diet. Men and women who exercise regularly tend to enjoy better physical and mental health. Modern medicine has proven that preventive measures especially if begun early seem to pay off in late life.

In some cases plans don't work out as we have planned. Neither partner may have a chance to care for the other because both become disabled and dependent almost at the same time. They may need help with some or all routine functions and personal care. They may need to turn to children who may be willing to help. However, much depends upon the relationship between generations and the ability to provide permanent care giving. The children may have their own health problems; their own children may need them or they may not have the financial and/or physical resources to create and sustain the necessary support system. In both the public and private sectors, economics underlie the ongoing shift to providing health and long term care in housing settings rather than institutional environments. This shift supports the living environment preference of older couples to stay where they are and "age in place." If there are sufficient funds as well as space, disabled couples may be able to remain where they are, hiring outside help for their care giving needs. However, when faced with insufficient funds and few employable caregivers, they may have to move to a long term care facility or into a child's home.

One of the greatest fears that older people have is of losing their independence and personal autonomy. The best way to allay these fears is to plan ahead, set clear goals, and let others know what these are. When a couple plans rather than drifts into their late life together, they may avoid many of the pitfalls lying in wait for those who grow old and have not made adequate preparations.

Before the mid century, health care was in the hands of a small cadre of physicians, surgeons, nurses, and technicians. The patient-physician relationship usually had a long personal history. This relationship was also predicated on the assumption that physicians, because of their training and expertise, knew what was best for patients, and that patients had an obligation to comply with physician advice.

Today health care is a giant industry with anonymous millions of care providers turning out a product to be used by consumers formerly known as patients. Health care providers often want and expect patients to be prepared to make decisions on their own behalf and take an active role in their own health care problems. Whether you are a patient or a partner, it is always in your best interest to be proactive and informed. As an advocate, one will have to assume a role somewhere between tiger and pussy cat depending upon your lifelong "historical or hysterical coping mechanisms." When this becomes a continuous process, the couple is better prepared to handle problems as they arise.

Married and heterosexual are the most common types of couples among middle-aged and older men and women. Yet, many older homosexual couples share a closed-couple relationship in which members tend to be sexually exclusive. This relationship most resembles heterosexual marriages in terms of strong emotional commitment and interdependence. Older gay and lesbian couples often consider themselves married in every sense of the word. Life partners are an essential part of gay and lesbian elders' support systems and need to be recognized for the importance they play in each others' lives.

The subject of gay and lesbian aging has gradually come out of the closet. At the same time, the oldest homosexuals – those in their 80s and beyond – remain largely invisible. After spending most of their lives in a world that offered them only bigotry and hatred, the vast majority have been averse to announcing their sexual preferences. Their experiences and concerns, therefore, have gone largely unacknowledged by younger members of their own community and only belatedly by the broader social community.

Who are older lesbians? What can these women teach a younger cohort about love relationships and sexuality to those who are poised to begin drawing their pensions? In *Whistling Women*, (2005) [14] Cheryl Claassen reflects on the life experiences of 44 lesbians aged 62 to 82. Half of the narrators were married (some for about 17 years or more), evidence of the compulsory heterosexuality pressure lesbians experienced in the 1940s and 50s. The personal stories show how historical events impacted on people's lives and how people are able to negotiate a space for themselves in trying situations such as "cultural invisibility."

In addition, several documentaries have been produced that profile the lives of older gays and lesbians. ***Golden Threads*** (1999) [15] directed by Lucy Winer and Karen Eaton, introduces viewers to Christine Burton, who at the age of 80 founded a national senior lesbians networking organization. ***Living with Pride: Ruth Ellis@100*** (1999)[16] profiles the life of a centenarian whose home was a gathering place for African American homosexuals in Detroit from the 1940s into the 1960s. The production highlights the central events that provide the background of the times plus Ellis' personal tales of her love life from a high school girl's crush on her gym teacher at 16 to a buoyant one-night stand at age 95.

Gay and Gray in New York City (1999) [17] is a thoughtful and well-researched video that features interviews with "gay and gray" men and women. It also profiles two organizations that work to provide services and support to the approximate 45,000 gay and lesbian seniors in New York City. Not having had role models of their own, these older homosexuals realize that they may be called upon to be role models for upcoming generations. "Nothing would please me more than to inspire young gay men and women to be themselves, whatever that happens to be," said one of the interviewees. "That's a legacy I would like to leave. "

Ruthie and Connie: Every Room in the House (2002) [18] is a film about two women in love and the price they pay to be themselves in mainstream society. Ruthie Berman and Connie Kurtz appear to be conventional housewives but their passionate interest in each other turns their world upside down. Overcoming many obstacles, their relationship spans 40 years of friendship and 25 years as loving partners.

The aging of the boomer generation is quietly drawing attention to another side of sexual intimacy, the part of the vows that pledges "in sickness," not only in health. In *Janet & Me: An Illustrated Story of Love and Loss,* [19] (2004) Stan Mack brings a poignant and fresh perspective to late life love and intimacy. The author uses a combination of text and drawings to pace the story along. Along the way, the couple lives their life together, experiencing the full range of coping, hoping, and care giving and grieving. Even when the news was as bad as it could be – when they were told Janet would never be cancer-free, there is a sense that this is not the end of them as a couple. The love of a good partner is forever.

Nowhere is the burden of care giving heavier than when one of the partners becomes permanently disabled and the other partner becomes the caregiver. Care giving is a stressful burden yet much depends upon the history of the couple's relationship and the subsequent physical and emotional changes that may have altered the relationship either in favor or against continued nurturance.

"I feel as if I'm sailing into darkness," British author Iris Murdoch murmurs uneasily to her husband John Bayley after learning that she is descending into Alzheimer's disease in the film *Iris* (2001).[20] However, Iris won't have to slide down into darkness alone. John, a literary critic, will stand with her every step of the way, tending to her needs, cajoling and stumbling through a heartbreaking landscape in which his brilliant and beloved wife is reduced to a silent, frightened child. Although the theme of the movie is the tragedy of Alzheimer's disease, a secondary and perhaps more powerful theme is the love and easy partnership that bound this eccentric and amazing couple together. John, the husband, is the glue that holds Iris together until her death.

Although sometimes the strain of protracted care giving can aggravate an already stormy relationship, occasionally, a disabling illness can smooth over the "rough edges" of conflicting personalities, allowing the healthy partner to become more caring while the disabled one is able to show gratitude for the unaccustomed concern. Regardless of the variety, patterns of care giving for irreversible conditions have one element in common--all lead to one inevitable final act.

In spite of the miraculous advances that have been made in medical technology, the increased availability of medical services, and a better standard of living for many people in the United States that has resulted in a considerably longer life expectancy in this century, death is still part of all human existence. Death is not abnormal; it comes to all living creatures. Yet, no one needs to be told that the death of a beloved partner is a tragic blow at any age, especially in late life.

Not only is extended couplehood a 21st century phenomena but its societal implications will reverberate in every area of human endeavor. These scouts together are treading on the unmarked beaches of an "age wave." Yet, the imprints they leave in the sand will not be washed away because some human values and needs never age. What remains constant is the need to communicate and the willingness to negotiate and adapt to each new stage. It is unrealistic to expect giant steps in change. What always matters is the way two people feel about one another and with that the hope that either or both partners will be willing to take even tiny steps in order to weather the challenges of later life together.

Unmarried women and unmarried men: Widowhood, divorce, dating, remarriage

© Mike Baldwin / Cornered

"The best things in life are free.
The rest are married."

A substantial number of older couples are formed in later life with the desire for companionship the motivating factor in their union. In *remarriage,* many couples are interested not only in romantic love but in companionship, lasting affection, and respect. They are not driven by hormones as they may have been earlier in their lives. They are even willing to risk alienating adult children by remarrying so as not to spend their last years alone. Playfulness, understanding, shared values and a desire for physical closeness are some of the factors that bring men and women together. *Used People* (1992)[2] is a movie set in Queens, New York in the '60s. Ethnic humor abounds in this story about the difficult romance between the sharp-tongued Jewish matriarch of a large family and the sweet-natured Italian gentleman who woos her from afar for 23 years.

The excitement of new love provides the adrenaline rush that people tend to equate with passion. The sexual attraction is as much a part of the relationship for an older couple as it is for two younger people. The novelty, the challenge, and the discovery are often the ingredients that make sex during this stage of a relationship incredibly exciting and are not exclusive to any one age, cohort, or sexual persuasion. In contrast to long-term relationships that allow for true sexual intimacy, some obvious sexual advantages are only experienced within the context of a new relationship. Older couples do report happiness in their second marriages.

However, in the following quote from Alex Comfort, we begin to understand what affects the continuity of a healthy sex life as people grow older.[3]

> *The best producer of an active and pleasurable sex life in the later years is an active and pleasurable sex life in the early years; the things that stop a person from having sex with increasing age are exactly the things that stop one from bicycle riding; bad health, thinking it looks silly, not having a bicycle. The difference is they happen later for sex than for bicycles.*

Why are there so many older men and women without bicycles? How are older widows and widowers adjusting to life without their partners? What about the single men and women who never had bicycles of their own? What about divorced people who have traded in their old models for different ones or are still shopping around? [4]

The odds of a marriage later in life favor single men more than single women. Older men live with their wives; older women live alone. That's because there are more single women than single men. A 60-year old man often can choose between women 35-60 while a 60-year-old woman often dates men 60 to 80.

To A Husband Who, After
Forty-Two Years, Dumped My
Wonderful Friend For A
Much Younger Woman

May you lose your state lottery ticket the day that you win.
May each meal that you eat leave a permanent stain
on your clothes.
May you get unsolicited telephone calls once a minute.
When you zip up your pants may your zipper get stuck
with it in it.

May you look in the mirror and shudder
at what you are seeing.
May your doctor prescribe colonoscopies ten times a year.
May your high school reunion class vote you
Least Loved Human Being.
May your chest get so droopy you need to go buy a brassiere.
May your days possess all the vibrancy of warm beer.
And throughout every night may you do far less sleeping
than peeing.

May your license expire and you flunk the exam to renew it.
May your dirtiest deeds be exposed in the national press.
May you find yourself trying to do it much more
than you do it.
May the answer to all of your prayers be a "no,"

not a "yes."
May you always be audited by the IRS.
And whenever you audit your life may you know that you blew it.[5]

—Judith Viorst 2000

Female longevity has consistently been the barrier to sexual activity for older women. Women live longer than men and have married men at least three years their senior. This means that a women may expect to live at least a decade as a widow. As the number of older singles increases, so do their options. ***Loners on Wheels*** (1998)[6] documents the life of a year round, singles-only, RV club, with a membership of over 4,000 adults. Edith Lane created this club almost thirty years ago because she was tired of being the only single traveler among couples. Defying the stereotype of single older men and women as outcasts, this portrait depicts older people filled with energy and spirit despite an average club member age of seventy. ***The Personals*** (1999)[7] follows a group of older men and women as they rehearse and present an original play at a community theater on Manhattan's Lower East Side. The play is structured around their quest for dates through the personal ads. The filmmaker follows these actors into their homes and presents viewers a humorous and in-depth portrait of the lives of older people in the U.S. today.

Thanks for the shared memories... And the opportunity to grow old together

Feature films and novels not only reflect society's conventions, but also help us to create them. In striving to differentiate stereotype from reality, we benefit not only from positive examples presented in the media, but also from questioning traditional concepts.

In ***The Book of Eve*** by Constance Beresford-Howe (1973)[8] the very week she receives her first old-age pension check, Eve walks out on her grouchy, demanding and insensitive invalid husband of 40 years. She surprises everyone with her instant decision. She also feels no remorse. Her first meeting with Johnny occurs when he tumbles down her basement stairs. Two "refugees" with a need for tenderness, romance and blissful sex have found one another.

Too Young to Die (2002)[9] is a South Korean romantic comedy between older widowers, Park Chi-Gyu, 72, and Lee Sun-ye, 71. After years of loneliness, they meet at a senior citizens' center, fall in love, and get married. He teaches his new wife how to read and she teaches him how to sing. As a couple, they rediscovered their sex life after 10 years of abstinence. The sex scenes in the movie emphasize the message that age does not matter in the pursuit of love and the fulfillment of one's sexuality.

The film *Foreign Affairs* (1993)[10] stars Joanne Woodward and Brian Dennehy. It is based on Alison Lurie's Pulitzer Prize-winning novel about the relationship between Vinnie and Chuck. They are two mature older adults with seemingly nothing in common. They meet on a trans-Atlantic flight in which Chuck keeps up a mostly one-sided conversation. During their stay in London, they keep running into each other to Chuck's delight and Vinnie's dismay. They fall in love. Woodward, in describing her enjoyment at portraying Vinnie said: "Just because you're over 60 doesn't mean that you might not have a romantic life. It's a good thing to show."

Shine (1992)[11] is a romantic comedy that focuses on the lives of two elderly and eccentric characters: Shine, a lonely widower and Eleanor, his new and feisty neighbor. This uneasy relationship between two older neighbors eventually heats up to a special night of mutual love and acknowledgement.

© Mike Baldwin / Cornered

"Lovely church. Do you do funerals?"

Although men often seek younger women, many younger men have no problem dating older women. Romance between older men and younger women has been so commonplace on-screen that the age difference often passes without comment. However, more women long instead for celebratory and inspiring tales of sexy older women. Unfortunately, such films have been few and far between. Hal Ashby's ***Harold and Maude*** (1971)[13] is the story of a shy and morose young man of 19 who meets a spunky older woman of 79 at a funeral. Maude feels he needs to come out of his shell and enjoy life, so she includes him in hers which is one long and unending series of lunatic adventures ranging from saving trees to grand theft auto. With her love and zest for life, Maude raises all manner of hormone levels and saves him from suicide. Their love affair is a tribute to life and spiritual enrichment for two of the least likely people to find one another. In another movie, ***How Stella Got Her Groove Back*** (1998)[14] is a splendid romance of a 40-year-old woman and 20-year-old man. Both film romances revolve around the couples' efforts to overcome obstacles to their coupling.

Today more and more older women find the men of their generation stuck in outdated non-egalitarian mode and younger cohorts of men more eager for gender equality. Real men want women of any age who like them, who want to make them feel good and who raise their testosterone level. An older woman often brings to bed a wealth of experience, confidence, competence and power that a younger woman can only dream of.

Ben Franklin, the multi-talented famous American, had a friend who did not want to get married but was very interested in female companionship. In the letter that follows, Franklin first advises his young friend to get married. However, since he realizes that his friend will not heed his advice, Franklin suggests that his friend have an affair with an older woman. Franklin's words about "putting a basket over her head," "turning out the light," or her "gratitude" for his manly favors are aspects of Franklin's character which are seldom described. Remember, too, that the letter was penned more than 300 years ago and less egalitarian attitudes towards women prevailed.

**Ben Franklin's Advice Concerning
His Friend's Sexual Affairs
June 25, 1745** [15]

My dear Friend,
   I know of no Medicine fit to diminish the violent natural Inclinations you mention; and if I did, I think I should not communicate it to you. Marriage is the proper Remedy. It is the most natural State of Man, and therefore the State in which you are most likely to find solid Happiness. Your Reasons against entering into it at present

appear to me not well-founded. The circumstantial Advantages you have in View by postponing it are not only uncertain, but they are small in comparison with that of the Thing itself, the being married and settled. It is the Man and Woman united that make the complete human Being. Separate, she wants his Force of Body and Strength of Reason; he, her Softness, Sensibility and acute Discernment. Together they are more likely to succeed in the World. A single Man has not nearly the Value he would have in that State of Union. He is an incomplete Animal. He resembles the odd half of a Pair of Scissors. If you get a prudent healthy Wife, your Industry in your Profession, with her good Economy, will be a Fortune sufficient.

But if you will not take this Counsel, and persist in thinking a Commerce with the Sex inevitable, then I repeat my former Advice, that in all your Amours you should prefer old Women to young ones. You call this a Paradox, and demand my Reasons. They are these:

1. Because as they have more Knowledge of the World and their Minds are better stored with Observations, their Conversation is more improving and more lastingly agreeable.

2. Because when Women cease to be handsome, they study to be good. To maintain their Influence over Men, they supply the Dimunition of Beauty by the Augmentation of Utility. They learn to do 1000 Services small and great, and are the most tender and useful of all Friends when you are sick. Thus they continue amiable. And hence there is hardly such thing to be found as an old Woman who is not a good Woman.

3. Because there is no hazard of Children, which irregularly produced may be attended with much Inconvenience.

4. Because through more Experience, they are more prudent and discreet in conducting and Intrigue to prevent Suspicion. The Commerce with them is therefore safer with regard to your Reputation. And with regard to theirs, if the Affair should happen to be known, considerate People might be rather inclined to excuse an old Woman who would kindly take care of a young Man, form his Manners by her good Counsels, and prevent his ruining his Health and Fortune among mercenary Prostitutes.

5. Because in every animal that walks upright, the Deficiency of the Fluids that fill the Muscles appears first in the highest Part: the Face grows lank and wrinkled; then the Neck; then the Breasts and Arms; the lower Parts continuing to the last as plump as ever: So that covering all above with a basket, and regarding only what is below the

Girdle, it is impossible of two Women to know an old from a young one. And as in the dark all Cats are grey, the Pleasure of corporal Enjoyment with an Old Woman is at least equal, and frequently superior, every Knack being of Practice capable of Improvement.

6. Because the Sin is less. The debauching of a Virgin may be her Ruin, and make her for Life unhappy.

7. Because the Compunction is less. The having made a young Girl miserable may give you frequent bitter Reflections; none of which can attend the making an old Women happy.

8. They are so grateful!!

Thus much for my Paradox. But still I advise you to marry directly; being sincerely Your affectionate Friend,

Benjamin Franklin

Many older women are taking a cue from celebrities who are linked with men who are years or even decades their junior. Many see themselves as the next Demi Moore and Ashton Kutcher or Susan Sarandon and Tim Robbins. These much publicized pairings acknowledge the growing acceptance of older women dating and living with younger men. A 2003 study by AARP The Magazine confirmed that more than a third of single women in the United States ages 40-69 are dating younger men.[16]

Late-life romantic relationships will likely increase because the Internet has made it easier for older singles to meet. Finding romance on the Internet is hardly new but it is on the upswing among people 55 and over. The Internet can be especially helpful to older women who as they age may not have the same dating opportunities as men. Online dating does have its drawbacks. The most common complaint: what you see online may not be what you get offline. Men and women lie about age and weight; some lie about marital status; photos may be old. Observers say one of the main obstacles to online dating for older subscribers was overcoming their technophobia, but that seems to be fading as more people use computers and the Internet.

Widowers and divorced older people often ask how long they should wait to get involved in a new relationship. It is different for each person but if they are interested they need to be visible and available. Getting back in the proverbial game once a good chunk of time has passed is an important step toward taking control of one's new life. And, with the right partner, life is just better.

Whether a couple chooses to marry becomes secondary to the desire for closeness and companionship that they seek. Older people form all sorts of relationships – from lunchtime partners to live-in companions to couples who marry. As Barbara Vinick, a sociologist with Boston University has said, "whether a couple is young or old, the euphoria and wanting to be with the other person is much the same."

The following feature article reprinted here provides a full and hopeful summary of the senior dating scene.

SEX, LIES AND VIAGRA:
DATING SCENE POSES A TANGLE OF ISSUES FOR OLDER SINGLES

Lara Adair

San Francisco Chronicle October 20, 2002[17]

Two women are toying with salads at a neighborhood restaurant and talking about – what else? – sex.

"I hate the part where I have to take off my clothes," says one. "I know I don't look as good as I used to."

"I don't either, Lord knows," says the other. "Lucky for us they don't see as well as they used to."

"It can be a lot of work, if you know what I mean," says the first. "They expect you to get them going."

"There are penile implants," her friend says, and the other nods. "Those do work."

Is this "Sex and the City," with Carrie and Miranda in their Manolo Blahniks and floaty tulle skirts together to rehash their sex lives?

Close. It's a Mill Valley restaurant where Arlene Davis, 65, and her lanky friend Evelyn Trainer, 70, in comfortable clothes and tennis shoes analyze their own dating scene: that of the suburban over-60 crowd. Davis is widowed and Trainer divorced, and both are interested in meeting men.

Their issues include those facing any singles, from where to meet people to who pays and how soon to fall into bed and whether or not to tie the knot. But they include issues unique to them, from what the children think to worries that their new love will die on them.

One person in 10 in this country is now older than 65, and many face old age alone. More than 70,000 single adults older than 60 have posted profiles on Match.com which has recently begun a site called SeniorMatch.Com tailored for older adults and easy to use.

Churches, synagogues, sports, volunteer activities bring people together the sure, but slow, way. Davis chose a personal ad in the Pacific Sun. Over the years she has met lots of men through her ad, which reads "Attractive widow, 61, seeking life companion."

"But you're 65," her friend points out.

"Everybody lies about their age," Davis says. She is slender with curly hair and a forthright manner. "I don't want to be discounted before I've even been met."

"Men lie, too," Trainer says. "They know women don't like old men who are probably winding down sexually and who could become incapacitated. You could be stuck at the bedside instead of in it."

Davis and Trainer have often met new partners at over-40 dances.

"Ours was the dance generation. Everyone could dance, and we went to dances all the time," says Trainer.

Now though, there are 10 women for every man at these gatherings, "so unfortunately most of the gals spend the evening holding up the wall, and only the aggressive ones get to dance," she says.

Davis counts herself among these. "I always ask the men to dance," she says.

"I don't like to sit. I've worked too hard not to have fun now."

Women, who usually handled the social calendar back when they were married, can more easily resume dating than men. But it evens out. Even the most bashful man finds himself a treasured commodity in this dating scene.

"Men who never had the opportunity to feel special in their lives can feel special just for having survived," says Myrna Lewis, co-author with Robert N. Butler of the popular book "The New Love and Sex After Sixty (Ballantine). The recently widowed man may find a brigade of women on his doorstep, eager to console him with a home-cooked meal, or these days, a lesson in how to get online.

Davis and Trainer say dating men their age has pluses and minuses. Older men can be courtly and have good manners, "but they are also used to making decisions," says Davis.

One of Davis' dates made a reservation at a Russian restaurant with a limited menu without finding out what kind of food she liked.

On another date, the man glanced at the menu and said grandly, "We'll have the Peking duck," without asking her what she wanted.

But when Davis, after making her date a long series of home-cooked meals asked him to pick up the dinner check, he suggested they split an entrée. "In our day men paid for everything, just for the delight of your company," says Trainer sighing.

Jim Lyle, a handsome 70-year-old bachelor in Lakeport, defends men's dating style. "With my Spartan budget, splitting checks is a must," he says. "I recently had a daylong date with a retired woman from out of town. She was interested in poetry readings, rock hunting and art, all bell-ringers for my interests. We started the day with breakfast (at my expense). Then we went to Copia in Napa, where I paid to enter, and for lunch. Next we went to the Napa Valley Art Museum (I paid the admission). Next, we went to the rock beds of the Russian River, where we found some jade, and finished the day with a meal at one of the mini-breweries before attending a poetry reading. Between meals, admissions and gas, I spent, in one day, over one-tenth of my monthly Social Security check. I did not ask her to pay, nor did she mention sex. She did call and thank me the nice day, though."

"The man may not have many interests, after a long marriage to one woman," Trainer says.

They are dismayed, she maintains, when a woman wants to talk about her children, and surprised when she wants to talk about politics.

"I want to explore ideas," Davis says, wistfully.

"Wait until the third date," counsels Trainer.

She adds:"Most women complain that the man talks about himself all the time and never inquires about the woman's interests. But weren't we all taught these moves long ago?

Always flatter the gentleman, be jolly and non-critical, and you'll probably get another date, if you want one."

Often older adults do want another date, because they seek love and intimacy.

According to the National Center on Longevity, 39% of seniors would like more sex than they're getting, and most men can still perform just fine, especially if their partner is patient. And Viagra? "A boon to older couples," says Lewis.

"People laugh about Viagra, Lyle says, "But I never had 'performance' problems until I started taking blood pressure medications. Then I did. Then Viagra became available (now, even through the Veterans Administration). No more problems other than the anticipation of preplanning as to when you take the pill. It does work, there is nothing strange, and I find nothing demeaning about taking one medicine to counter the side effects of another."

The women say they want cuddling and closeness. "Touching people is important," says Davis.

This crowd is not used to taking precautions or swapping sexual histories, but, according to Lewis, rates of HIV are rising for people older than 60.

"All of us in this field recommend anybody who starts dating again be thoughtful about HIV," Lewis says. "We've known women in their 80s who've gotten HIV from sexual contact. Women think, 'I don't have anything to worry about, because he was married all those years,' but who knows what he was up to?"

Sometimes, older people entering new relationships are not eager to share their new joy with their children. Davis brings her cell phone with her when she stays with a boyfriend in case her daughter calls. The kids can be judgmental or hostile to a new love interest out of fear of being disinherited ("the will watchers," Lewis call them.).

Or, in the case of the frail elderly, they can worry about their parents being taken advantage of by more sophisticated or predatory partners.

Like many older people, Davis and Trainer are financially independent, own their own homes and do not see marriage as a goal. It would be a headache to work out new wills, new beneficiaries.

"Women can be ambivalent about remarrying, especially if they've been the caretaker for their dying husband," Lewis says. "A number of widows say, 'Never again!' at the thought of seeing another person through their dying days. Increasingly what we will see are two independent adults who simply live together, keeping their financial lives separate."

"I'm not looking for support," Davis says. "I love running my own life. I'm just looking for a solid emotional connection."

Chances are good she will find it. Both women have friends in close and satisfying relationships. Davis has, in fact, a date that very night, with a man who has already sent a bouquet of roses.

Intimacy:
In the community and in long term care...

Most health care professionals have been taught little about aging and sexuality. Therefore, sexual history is often overlooked in social service and health care settings. Many care providers are unable and/or unwilling to acknowledge the importance of sex in their patients'/clients' lives and, as a result, fail to address their sexual concerns. They often fall prey to the same ageist stereotypes and attitudes about love and intimacy among older adults that are prevalent in our society.

Most primary care physicians are not adequately trained in men's and women's sexual responses, the medications that may impede these responses, or appropriate treatment options. Older patients are often placed on a medical regimen without taking a careful sexual health history or without asking them if they wish to continue an active sex life. Moreover, gynecologists are not usually consulted. Medical problems and medications can interfere with sexual functioning. Bouts of depression, anxiety, grief, disappointment, or shame may compromise the older person's self-perception and sense of sexuality. In order to provide quality health care, providers need to be much more frank about raising sexual issues with their older patients.

Even care providers who are not trained experts in the issues of sexual health can provide help and support by minimally expanding what they are already trained to do: assess and evaluate; and, treat and/or refer. Often the issue of sexuality is just beneath the surface when an older person talks of love or loneliness. By simply initiating a discussion of sexual concerns, the care provider may often be offering the most valuable component of treatment for patients and their partners. By addressing issues of sexuality, the physician informs the patient that it is appropriate to discuss sexual problems in that setting; it validates the patient's self-perception as a sexual being. The care provider cannot provide an effective intervention if there is no mention of a problem. They can play an instrumental role in encouraging the continuation of sexual expression for those who need such support. As human beings, we are also sexual beings; thus, there are problems related to sexuality that could affect other parts of our total being.

Likewise, the professional needs to be mindful that some older people do not want to engage in any sexual activity. Care providers must not put undue pressure upon them to be sexually active or to even discuss sexuality if they are not so inclined. This should be respected; however, many people will welcome the opportunity for supportive help. Most will generally be appreciative to know that a professional is willing and able to discuss the issues.

Health care and social service providers can be instrumental in providing guidance, education, and acceptance. What an older person may want most when he or she raises sexual concerns is acknowledgement and support. Sharing educational information regarding sexual functioning in older people can be useful only if the person is emotionally ready to listen. Cooperation with medical resources in clarifying medical restrictions on sexual behavior, if any, can be reassuring to the older person who might be frightened and reluctant to ask.

Communication is the key; the professional needs to use clear, unambiguous language. Using words like "sexual intercourse" and "masturbation" may give the patient the tacit permission to use these words, too. It is invaluable to the dialogue that the professional be familiar with the verbal and nonverbal expressions used to discuss sexuality in the context of the older person's comfort level. Professionals working with older men and women need to be aware of the cultural, religious, and social forces that influence their own value systems in order to better comprehend the multiple factors at work affecting the value systems of their older patients. Closely related to the above, professionals need to be mindful that they not impose current cultural expectations about sexual expression upon older patients who may not be able to overcome a lifetime of sexual misinterpretations and prohibitions.

Despite our sexually enlightened culture, many older couples still hold onto fairly restrictive and conservative views of what is "appropriate" and "normal." Therefore, the health care provider's role as educator would be to help older patients redefine what "normal" sexual activity entails. A couple may be having difficulty realizing sexual satisfaction due to genital atrophy or erectile dysfunction. A care provider could explore with them the possibility of moving away from the standard missionary position and intercourse and towards different positions and ways of stimulation (increased use of oral sex, manual stimulation, sexual aids, and sensual non-genital activities like bathing together, massage or erotic movies/literature).

Change does not have to be extreme for couples to notice significant improvement in sexual fulfillment. It may imply something as simple as suggesting that couples make love in the morning when older people have more energy rather than late in the evening when there is a greater likelihood of fatigue. Furthermore, it is important to remind older couples to learn to communicate better both in and out of the bedroom. As their sexual repertoire requires some adjustment or change, a couple needs to learn how to communicate in order to smoothly accomplish this.

Many older persons maintain a desire to continue or initiate sexual activity yet an acceptable partner may not be available. Men may have multiple opportunities for sexual partners whereas women, with the uneven ratio of older men to older women, may have very few. Older men are more likely to be married and older women are more likely to be widowed, thus affecting the opportunities for sexual expression in an ongoing, intimate relationship.

Providing older adults in long term care facilities an opportunity to express their sexuality presents a special challenge to physical and mental health providers. Only five percent of our population resides in nursing homes or skilled care facilities at any one time.

However, over ten percent can expect to be in such a facility at some point in their lives. The lack of privacy often presents an obstacle to sexual expression for older residents in these facilities. Living arrangements do not automatically place spouses in the same room, often because of different levels of care. Facilities may not be equipped to offer spouses or unmarried partners the private space for conjugal visits. The lack of privacy may simply be the reality of limited space in an already crowded facility or the intentional decision of the staff not to provide such space due to the wishes of adult children about their family members, an institutional decision not to address these issues, or a religious affiliation that discourages sexual relations between unmarried persons. Sometimes, too, since the continuing sexuality of older people is often an uncomfortable reality for long-term care staff members, some staff may demean older residents by teasing or ridiculing them when they express physical desire towards another resident.

Long term care residents, in general, tend to be the most powerless, voice-less, and invisible groups in our society. Doris Hammond, a researcher in sexuality and aging, has suggested that residents in long term care facilities have a greater need than other older adults for sexual intimacy.[1] Having experienced so many cumulative losses related to disability, widowhood, finances, social roles, etc., emotional closeness can be of considerable benefit to a resident's self-esteem. Encouragement can be given by helping residents to dress more attractively thus supporting their masculine or feminine identity. When residents feel good about themselves, they also feel better about one another. Residents with a more positive outlook trigger more resident-appropriate behavior from staff. However, it is necessary to understand, too, that there are sometimes circumstances when open sexual expression in an institutional setting is not appropriate and staff will intervene to curb or redirect inappropriate sexual advances.

More Than Skin Deep (2001)[2] is a video set against the backdrop of a nursing home beauty shop. Through the stories and insights of nursing home residents, it examines issues of self-esteem and aging; and, it takes an evocative look at the connections between living well, aging with dignity, and looking good.

The Heart Has No Wrinkles (2004)[3] presents the love story of May and Derek, elderly residents of a nursing home. The video combines interviews and a realistic dramatic situation that emphasizes that even though the relative importance of sexuality in a relationship may change, it remains an essential part of each individual's life. The need for love, respect, and intimacy does not diminish with age.

Rose by Any Other Name (2003)[4] is a film about the older person's search for closeness, privacy and love as presented in the relationship between Rose Gordon and Mr. Morris, both residents of a nursing home. The administration and staff of the home, Mrs. Gordon's family and the institutional nature of long-term care, however, threaten this relationship. The film explores the reactions of other people to a loving relationship that appears "unseemly." The film is designed to help older people, their families, and those in policy-making positions develop informed judgments about the lifelong needs for love and sexual intimacy.

The long term care resident is usually a woman because of different life expectancy between men and women. Since men die younger, they are usually ill at home and being taken care of by their spouse. When the wife falls ill and lacks a social support network, she may need to rely on the care provided by a long term care facility. The following poem by Donna Swanson is a tribute to older women residing in long term care facilities who share a fundamental yet often unfulfilled human need for physical and emotional affirmation.

Minnie Remembers

> God; My hands are old.
> I've never said that out loud
> before but they are.
> I was so proud of them once.
> They were soft like the velvet
> smoothness of a firm, ripe peach.
> Now the softness is more life worn-
> out sheets or withered leaves.

When did these slender, graceful
hands become gnarled,
shrunken claws? When, God?
They lie here in my lap,
naked reminders of this worn-out
body that has served me too well!
How long has it been since
someone touched me?
Twenty years?
Twenty years I've been a widow.
Respected. Smiled at.
But never touched.
Never held so close that
loneliness was blotted out.
I remember how my mother used
to hold me, God.
When I was hurt in spirit or flesh,
she would gather me close,
stroke my silky hair and caress
my back with her warm hands.
O God: I'm so lonely.
I remember the first boy who ever
kissed me.
We were both so new at that!
The taste of young lips and
popcorn, the feeling inside
of mysteries to come.
I remember Hank and the babies
How else can I remember them
but together?
Out of the fumbling, awkward
attempts of new lovers

came the babies.
And as they grew, so did our love
And, God, Hank didn't seem to
mind, if my body thickened
and faded a little.
He still loved it. And touched it.
And we didn't mind if we were no
longer beautiful.
And the children hugged me a lot.
O God, I'm lonely!
God, why didn't we raise the kids
to be silly and affectionate
as well as dignified and proper?
You see, they do their duty.
drive up in their fine cars:
they come to my room
to pay their respects.
They chatter brightly, and
reminisce.
But they don't touch me.
They call me "Mom" or "Mother" or
"grandma."
Never Minnie.
My mother called me Minnie.
So did my friends.
Hank called me Minnie, too.
But they're gone.
And so is Minnie.
Only Grandma is here.
And God! She's lonely![5]

—*Donna Swanson 1978*

Caretakers and administrators in long term care settings are finding that more and more residents are seeking out and engaging in sexual expression which includes words, gestures, or activities that appear to be motivated by a need for sexual gratification. More facilities are finding that there is more intimacy among residents regardless of living arrangements and mental or marital status. Even those residents suffering from dementias are capable of romantic attachments and sexual feelings. However, these attachments often raise personal and ethical questions that pit individual rights against family values. In addition, there are still gray areas when it comes to the prevalence of dementia in the aging population and issues of privacy and consent. *A Thousand Tomorrows: Intimacy, Sexuality and Alzheimer's* (1995)[6] uses candid interviews with several Alzheimer's disease patients and their spouse caregivers to examine a number of issues surrounding how the disease affects intimacy and sexuality. The video describes the changes in behavior that affect intimacy between the partners, and the mismatch of sexual desire and attraction.

Some facilities have begun to have staff discussions and role playing in order to examine the meaning of the behavior of "the dirty old man" and "the shameless old woman." Some have also counseled families, especially adult children about the sexual needs of their parents. In other facilities, caring for live pets has given residents the opportunity to care for, hold and stroke a live pet. This enhances a person's sexuality through the touching and closeness that occurs; it provides a living thing to care for. Other facilities have experimented with providing opportunity for touching, i.e., more hugging, kissing, hand-holding. In addition they have incorporated back rubs and body massages in their programs. Touch is the quintessential human gift at both the beginning and the end of life. No one is too ill that they would not find some aspect of physical touch soothing and comforting.

The Hebrew Home for the Aged in Riverdale, New York has continuously been in the forefront for addressing major issues related to long term care. In 1995, the Home introduced a set of policies and procedures concerning sexual expression among the residents. The policy states that "residents have the right to seek out and engage in sexual expression." It encourages intimacy and positive physical touching. It prohibits relationships with minors, public displays and nonconsensual acts. An explicit training video was created to educate staff on how to deal with sexual rights and needs of their residents. The video has been shown in connection with an educational training program at other like institutions. Below is a reprint of an article describing the Hebrew Home for the Aged in Riverdale and the perceptions of residents and care providers on sexual intimacy in a long term care residence.

A Sexual Revolution For The Elderly[7]
At Nursing Homes, Intimacy Is Becoming a Matter of Policy
Matthew Purdy

They met last New Year's Eve. He was tall with an easy manner. She was petite with a girlish smile. He asked her to dance and held her close. "I didn't push him away," she said. "I've been around awhile. I've pushed a lot of men away."

It was a modern romance, at once pure and complicated. First, there was his wife. He was still married, although separated. Then, there was his walker.

Fritzie Heilbron's prince came to her not astride a white horse, but in black orthopedic shoes, shuffling along with the help of a walker. He is 76 years old, impaired by Parkinson's disease, and with enough fear of his wife to want his name kept private. But Mrs. Heilbron is smitten. She's 85 and has waited 45 years since her husband died to fall in love again.

This is not a case of geriatrics going clubbing. It is a scene from a nursing home, where those who care for the elderly and infirm report a kind of sexual revolution. The revolution is not among the elderly, who experts say have always demonstrated an enduring urge for intimacy, but in the attitude of those who provide care. They are beginning to recognize that sexual activity is normal and beneficial for patients – even for those with Alzheimer's disease.

At the Hebrew Home for the Aged, a 1,200-bed nursing home and Alzheimer's research center in the Riverdale section of the Bronx where Mrs. Heilbron and her companion found each other, a new policy gives patients the right to privacy so they can carry on intimate relationships. In confronting the issue directly, the Hebrew Home is in the vanguard of the shift away from seeing sex in nursing homes as a behavior problem.

The home is training its staff to recognize and respect intimate relationships, and officials there say they will try to assist budding romances by moving one member of a couple to a single room to provide privacy.

"A couple of years ago, when there were people who were sexually involved, we thought we had to separate them," said Robin Bouru, a social worker at the Hebrew Home.

Because most nursing home residents share rooms, some homes around the country have set aside rooms that couple can use for privacy, and others have formalized policies for addressing sexual activity, like the one at the Hebrew Home. But Meredith Wallace, a geriatric nurse who has written about sexuality of the aged, said many homes are moving slowly, if at all, to break down "the old stereotypes."

Antonette Zeiss, a clinical psychologist at the Veterans Administration Health Care system in Palo Alto, California, who has instructed nursing home administrators in California on sexual relations among patients, said the subject is difficult to confront because "it's the conjunction of two taboos about sex." "The first," she said, "is that sex is for the young. The second is that sex is for the cognitively intact."

She said that in her experience most people who run nursing homes agree that residents have a right to sexual expression, but it is difficult for staff members to support "because they feel uncomfortable with it."

Others have raised more straightforward objections, from the danger of patients physically hurting themselves to the violation of moral laws at homes that are run by religious organizations.

Janet Lowe, a nurse's aide at the Hebrew Home, said that the first time she realized two unwed residents were having a relationship, "I was shocked. You don't think of your grandparents having sex." Ms. Lowe said other members of the staff had stronger objections. "Some people thought it should be stopped because they weren't married."

Jacob Reingold, the vice chairman of the Hebrew Home, which is run according to Orthodox Jewish law, acknowledges that the home would face a quandary if two unwed patients wanted to live together as a couple.

For many at the Hebrew Home, romance is a welcome relief from the unbroken landscape of aches and pains and dwindling days. "I think it's beautiful, seeing a man and a woman walking together holding hands," said Ethel Hoberman, who is 81, healthy, spry and available. "It sort of gives the place the feeling of being alive, rather than waiting to die."

Some staff members and residents find the sexual relationships between unwed, elderly people immoral or distasteful, or both. "There are some women who say: 'Yuck, that's disgusting. They're going to give them rooms so they can do things there?" said Grace Meltzer, a resident of the Hebrew Home.

Sonya Kantor, who is 86 and president of the residents' council at the home, discreetly said, "I have a gentleman friend here" and explained the negative comments this way: "The disapproval of some of the women may come from the fact that they don't have male friends."

Officials at the Hebrew Home said intimate relationships return some dignity to residents who give up privacy and freedom in exchange for assistance and security. "Can't we allow them to have some vestige of normalcy in this critical area?" said Douglas Holmes, a psychologist who heads the home's research division. "I'm totally pro-sex as long as no one is victimized."

The thorniest issue of sexual conduct at nursing homes involves relations between patients with dementia.

Psychologists and doctors say aberrant behavior like public masturbation and unwanted kissing and touching of others is common with Alzheimer's patients, who often lose the ability to make social judgments. But, said Dr. Philip D. Sloane, a professor at the University of North Carolina medical school who advises the Manor Health Care chain of 170 nursing homes on Alzheimer's care, "a lot of time, the activity we think of as sexually deviant behavior is just reaching out for intimacy."

Like the Hebrew Home, the Manor Health Care homes have a protocol for evaluating instances where patients with dementia exhibit a strong attraction. He said it is not unusual for the staff, in conjunction with a resident's family, to allow casual intimacy – holding hands, hugging – but that sex is rarely if ever allowed, out of concern for the patients' safety and the difficulty of determining whether they consent.

At the Hebrew Home, Mrs. Meltzer, who lives on a different floor than her husband because he suffers from dementia, said even in his confused state his need for closeness emerges.

"I think intimate sex is the farthest thing from his mind," she said. "He reaches for my hand and kisses me. And he says why don't you get undressed and get into bed. I think he just wants intimacy."

Mrs. Meltzer said the need for companionship doesn't fade with age. She said that when she first moved to the home she was told about a man who was found naked and dead in the bed of a woman who lives there. Mrs. Meltzer said she still remembered her reaction: "I said, 'Well, anyway, he died happy.'"

The best is yet to come,
and won't that be fine... [1]

Frank Sinatra

Age is frequently overused and misused. Irrational prejudice often occurs in judging a person's capabilities on the basis of the characteristics of a conditioned age group and what we presume as being appropriate and typical of that age set. Society has made assumptions about aging that are now outdated. Perhaps these assumptions were useful at one time, like old wives' tales, but today they no longer serve a purpose.

Myths and stereotypes permeate the subject of love and sex among older adults. These myths have enshrined conservative social values and have often been used to confirm rather than explain or question cultural attitudes and norms.[2]

Since people are prone to act as they are expected, societal expectations that older people should not feel or exhibit romantic and sexual interest often meant that older people prematurely refrained from continuing, developing and sharing loving intimate relations and pursuing sexual activity. As we get older, personal relationships take on increased importance. Sexual intimacy is a way to reaffirm the love of life. It expresses the closeness of our deepest relationships and is an important measure of quality of life.

The good news is that as Baby Boomers age, they are likely to impact ageist attitudes just as they are now impacting nearly every aspect of aging. A more liberated attitude about love and sex, the sheer number of Baby Boomers in the current cohort and an increase in the life expectancy of both men and women suggest that elder sexuality will become a more accepted norm by older persons, their grown children, and society at large. The Senior Boomers are likely to be more comfortable expressing their sexuality than previous cohorts who were influenced by stricter religious and societal taboos. Baby Boomers' focus on physical fitness, anti-aging regimens and physical attractiveness will also affect how sexuality in older people will be expressed, viewed and accepted. In addition, they will acknowledge sexuality as a continuation of normal lifelong pleasures and as a quality of life issue central to health promotion and well-being.

Everyone should experience a lifetime of positive, ongoing sexuality if that is his/her inclination. It is one of the most unique aspects of life and should be understood and enjoyed throughout a person's life. While many factors may affect sexuality as people age, even the most serious conditions seldom prohibit participation in sexual activity. Most older people experience interest in sexual intimacy. Many people are sexually intimate well into their 80s and beyond since our capacity for sexual intimacy will be with us our entire lives.

Attitudes and psychological outlook, more than physical limitations, will determine a person's ability to achieve sexual satisfaction. The foundation of sexual intimacy throughout the life cycle, however, will not be found in mastery of specific sexual skills. The real difference in sexual intimacy is the way sexuality is expressed. Most anything can be a turn-on at 20, but at 60, after years of sexual experience, expressions of sexuality are more refined, more evolved. The act can at this time be a masterwork after years of study. It will be achieved by those with the ability to give and receive love, and to cherish and be cherished by their partner.

The greatest thing you'll ever learn
is just to love and be loved in return...
—Nat King Cole (*"Nature Boy"*)[4]

Endnotes

Cover: Photo courtesy www.elissa.org/2001

The fires still burn…

1. Doris Hammond, *My Parents Never Had Sex,* Prometheus Books, Buffalo, New York, 1987.
2. Erich Fromm, *The Art of Loving*, New York, Harper & Row, 1956.
3. The Beatles (Lennon/McCartney). *All You Need is Love*. United Kingdom, 1967.
4. Lois Wyse, Yes in *Love Poems for the Very Married*. World Publishers New York, 1967. Renewed 1995. Reprinted by permission HarperCollins, NewYork.
5. Annie Dillard, *The Living,* New York, Harper-Collins, 1992.
6. Mary Ellen Mark, *Esther and Al Kline in their apartment, Miami Beach, Florida.* Catalogue number: 201H-001-016. Used with permission.
7. Pierre Teilhard de Chardin, *The Heart of Matter.* William Collins Sons & Co. &Harcourt, 1978.
8. C.B. White, *A Scale for the Assessment of Attitude and Knowledge Regarding Sexuality in the Aged.* Archives of Sexual Behavior 11 (1982): 491-502. Reprinted by permission.

What I thought I knew about love and sex and really don't...

1. Gabriel Garcia Marquez, *Love in the Time of Cholera.* New York, Penguin, 1988

2. Vatsayayana, *The Complete Illustrated Kama Sutra.* Lance Dane (editor). Inner Traditions Bear & Company, 2003.

3. Alfred Kinsey, *Sexual Behavior in the Human Male* (original 1948). Indiana University Press, 1998

4. Alfred Kinsey, *Sexual Behavior of the Human Female.* (original 1953). Indiana University Press, 1998.

5. Cartoon Stock Cartoons, license Category 4;jba0009. Used by permission.

6. Cartoon Stock Cartoons, license Category 4; jba0017. Used by permission.

7. Henry Wadsworth Longfellow, Morituri Salutamus: Poem for the Fiftieth Anniversary of the Class of 1825 in Bowdoin College in: *The Poetical Works of Henry Wadsworth Longfellow,* Boston & New York, Houghton-Mifflin, 1890.

8. CartoonStock Cartoons, license Category 4; grin222. Used by permission.

9. The National Council on the Aging (September, 1998). Healthy Sexuality and Vital Aging. www.cin-ncoa.org/love/natural_part.htm.

10. Pfizer Global Study of Sexual Attitudes and Behaviors, 2002.

11. Alex Comfort, *The Joy of Sex,* New York, Simon & Schuster, 1974.

12. Niki Nymark, *When the Old Folks Make Love,* 2002. Reprinted by permission.

Women's mid-life journey: If not now, then when...?

1. Thomas Mann, *The Black Swan.* Alfred A. Knopf, New York, 1954.

2. Dori Appel, Meaning Menopause in: *Women of the 14th Moon.* Crossing Press, Santa Cruz, California,.1991. Reprinted by permission.

3. Barbara Myerhoff, *Number Our Days.* Simon & Schuster (Touchstone), New York, 1978.

4. Ken Dychtwald, *Age Wave.* Bantam Books, New York, 1988.

5. *Pirke Avot,* The Sayings of the Ancestors [Hillel].

6. Simone de Beauvoir, *The Second Sex.* Alfred A. Knopf, New York, 1953.

7. Germaine Greer, *The Change: Women, Aging and the Menopause.* Ballantine Books,

New York, 1991.

8. *Antonia's Line*. First Line Pictures, 1995.

9. *Like Water for Chocolate*. Miramax, 1992.

10. Doris Lessing, *The Golden Notebook*. Simon & Schuster, New York, 1962.

11. Mapie, 1999. http://txc.net.au/-mapie/midlifecrisisforwomen.htm

12. *Pirke Avot,* The Sayings of the Ancestors [Rabbi Tarfon].

Marriage: Growing older together

1. Barbara Silverstone and K.H.Hyman. *Growing Older Together.* Pantheon, New York, 1992.

2. Khalil Gibran, *The Prophet.* Alfred A Knopf, New York, 1923.

3. *The Notebook*, New Line Cinema, 2004.

4. Judity Viorst, About His Retirement in *Suddenly Sixty and other shocks of later life..* Simon & Schuster, New York, 2000. Reprinted by permission of Lescher & Lescher, Ltd. All rights reserved.

5. Finnegan Alford-Cooper. *For Keeps: Marriages that Last a Lifetime.* M.E. Sharpe, 1998.

6. Lois Wyse, Non-Stop, in *Love Poems for the Very Married.* World Publishing, New York, 1967. Renewed 1995. Reprinted by permission HarperCollins Publishers, New York

7. Larry Kohler & Harry Mann (words and music), *I Love How You Love Me.* © 1961 (Renewed 1989) SCREEN GEMS-EMI MUSIC, INC. All Rights Reserved. International Copyright Secured. Used by permission.

8. *China,* PBS drama, 2003.

9. Lois Wyse, Half-Squeezed, in *Love Poems for the Very Married.* (see above).

10. *As Time Goes By*, PBS distributed British television series, 1992-2005.

11. Barry W. McCarthy. *Getting it Right the First Time*, England, Brenner-Routledge Press, 2004.

12. Helen Fisher. *Why We love: The Nature and Chemistry of Romantic Love.* New York, Henry Holt, 2004.

13. Lorraine Dorfman and D. Heckert. Egalitarianism in Retired Rural Couples: Household

Tasks, Decision- Making, and Leisure Activities. *Family Relations*. 37(1988):73-8.

14. Cheryl Claassen, *Whistling Women: A Study of the Lives of Older Lesbians*. New York, Haworth Press, 2005.

15. *Golden Threads*, (video), 1999.

16. *Living with Pride: Ruth Ellis@100*. Wolfe Video, 1999.

17. *Gay and Gray in New York City*. Fanlight Productions, 1999.

18. *Ruthie and Connie: Every Room in the House* (video), 2002.

19. Stan Mack, *Janet & Me: An Illustrated Story of Love and Loss*. New York, Simon & Schuster, 2004.

20. *Iris*. Miramax, 2001.

Unmarried women and unmarried men:
Widowhood, divorce, dating, remarriage

1. CartoonStock Cartoons, license category 4;mban 1594. Used by permission.

2. *Used People*. 20th Century Fox, 1992.

3. Alex Comfort, (see above).

4. Doris Hammond (see above).

5. Judith Viorst, To A Husband Who, After Forty-Two Years, Dumped My Wonderful Friend For A Much Younger Woman in *Suddenly Sixty and other shocks of later life* (see above).

6. *Loners on Wheels*. New Road Films, 1998.

7. *The Personals*. Fanlight Productions, 1999.

8. Constance Beresford-Howe, *The Book of Eve*. Canada, New Canadian Library, 1973.

9. *Too Young to Die*. Toronto International Film Festival, 2002.

10. *Foreign Affairs*. Turner Home Entertainment, 1993.

11. *Shine*. Library Media Project, 1992.

12. CartoonStock Cartoons, license category 4; mban125. Used by permission.

13. *Harold and Maude*. Paramount Pictures, 1971.

14. *How Stella Got Her Grove Back*. 20th Century Fox, 1998.

15. Benjamin Franklin's Advice Concerning His Friend's Sexual Affairs from *Advice to a Young Man*, Philadelphia, June 25, 1745.

16. Xenia Montenegro, *Lifestyles, Dating and Romance: A Study of Midlife Singles*. AARP, 2003.

17. Lara Adair. Sex, lies and Viagra: Dating Scene Poses a Tangle of Issues for Older Singles in *San Francisco Chronicle,* October 20, 2002. Used by permission.

Intimacy: In the community and in long term care

1. Doris Hammond (see above).

2. *More Than Skin Deep.* Fanlight Productions, 2001.

3. *The Heart Has No Wrinkles.* Terra Nova films, 2004.

4. *Rose by Any Other Name.* Judith Keller, 2003.

5. Donna Swanson, Minnie Remembers in *Mind Song.* Nashville, Tennessee, Upper Room, 1978.

6. *A Thousand Tomorrows: Intimacy, Sexuality and Alzheimer's.* Terra Nova Films, 1995.

7. Matthew Purdy. A Sexual Revolution for The Elderly in *The New York Times*, November 6, 1995, p. A14. Used by permission.

The best is yet to come, And won't that be fine... [1]

1. Frank Sinatra. The best is yet to come, and won't that be fine in *Sinatra Reprise: The Very Good Years.* 1991.

2. Ann Oakley, *Woman's Work: The Housewife, Past and Present*, New York, Pantheon, 1975.

3. gettyimages.com Image 200116663-005. Used by permission.

4. Nat King Cole. Nature Boy in *Nat King Cole – The Greatest Hits,* Capitol,1994.